TRANS

QUICK TAKES: MOVIES AND POPULAR CULTURE

Quick Takes: Movies and Popular Culture is a series offering suc-
cinct overviews and high-quality writing on cutting-edge themes
and issues in film studies. Authors offer both fresh perspectives
on new areas of inquiry and original takes on established topics.

SERIES EDITORS:

Gwendolyn Audrey Foster is Willa Cather Professor of English
and teaches film studies in the Department of English at the University of Nebraska, Lincoln.

Wheeler Winston Dixon is the James Ryan Endowed Professor of Film Studies and professor of English at the University of
Nebraska, Lincoln.

Rebecca Bell-Metereau, *Transgender Cinema*
Blair Davis, *Comic Book Movies*
Steven Gerrard, *The Modern British Horror Film*
Barry Keith Grant, *Monster Cinema*
Daniel Herbert, *Film Remakes and Franchises*
Ian Olney, *Zombie Cinema*
Valérie K. Orlando, *New African Cinema*
Stephen Prince, *Digital Cinema*
Dahlia Schweitzer, *L.A. Private Eyes*
Steven Shaviro, *Digital Music Videos*
David Sterritt, *Rock 'n' Roll Movies*
John Wills, *Disney Culture*

Transgender Cinema

REBECCA BELL-METEREAU

RUTGERS UNIVERSITY PRESS

New Brunswick, Camden, and Newark, New Jersey, and London

Library of Congress Cataloging-in-Publication Data
Names: Bell-Metereau, Rebecca Louise, author.
Title: Transgender cinema / Rebecca Bell-Metereau.
Description: New Brunswick : Rutgers University Press, [2019] |
Includes index. | Includes bibliographical references
and filmography.
Identifiers: LCCN 2018031135 | ISBN 9780813597331 (paperback) |
ISBN 9780813597348 (cloth)
Subjects: LCSH: Transgender people in motion pictures.
Classification: LCC PN1995.9.T684 B45 2019 |
DDC 791.43/653—dc23
LC record available at https://lccn.loc.gov/2018031135

A British Cataloging-in-Publication record for this book is
available from the British Library.

∞ The paper used in this publication meets the requirements of
the American National Standard for Information Sciences—
Permanence of Paper for Printed Library Materials,
ANSI Z39.48-1992.

www.rutgersuniversitypress.org

Manufactured in the United States of America

CONTENTS

PREFACE

As a cisgender scholar who has examined issues of gender and androgyny for over three decades, I am an enthusiastic ally of the trans community. I also realize that I view these films primarily from the perspective of film reception, and parts of this study tread into some categorical mine fields, rife with potential ideological disputes. I approach this mission with humility and advance apologies for any blunders or omissions I make in describing the artistic vision of transgender filmmakers and actors, along with the work of nontransgender actors and filmmakers whose works depict the lives and experiences of the transgender community. This work explores what constitutes trans cinema and when it first emerged, where we can locate it, why we need to study it, and how to best explore and analyze this rich body of work in a concise introductory way. I look forward to the lively dialogue, critiques, and ongoing discovery inherent in any relatively new field of study. I have relied on scholars, popular writers, and members of the transgender community for various perspectives, in an effort to explore the production and reception of these works and artists among a variety of audiences. I hope to contribute some small part to our cultural understanding of the lives and artistic goals of this groundbreaking creative community.

TRANSGENDER CINEMA

INTRODUCTION

LGBTQ and trans communities have been peeping through the cracks and windows of popular movies for glimpses of themselves since the turn of the nineteenth century, when Charlie Chaplin dressed as a beautiful woman in *The Masquerader* (1914). Decades later, Jennifer Livingston documented the Harlem drag-ball scene in *Paris Is Burning* (1990), Tilda Swinton and the director Sally Potter adapted Virginia Woolf's literary transgender *Orlando* (1992) for the screen, Hilary Swank reenacted the real-life struggles of Teena Brandon to become Brandon Teena in Kimberly Peirce's *Boys Don't Cry* (1999), and in the next century, Sophie Hyde's *52 Tuesdays* (2013) showed an adolescent girl adapting to her mother's transition to being male over the course of a year. These representative works constitute only a tiny fraction of films that depict some aspect of transgender experience. Interest in trans figures goes beyond the LGBTQ community, as some 159,000 results from a 2018 Google search for "transgender film" would indicate.

In spite of this nascent emergence of trans perspectives onscreen, powerful members of society continue to resist change and attempt to suppress the community in a variety of ways. For example, politicians in 2016 and 2017 drafted laws to turn back the clock in North Carolina and Texas, debating discriminatory bathroom bills aimed at forcing conformity to gender identity as designated on birth certificates. This political repression was not the only conflict over a community that has already changed attitudes in industrialized nations and promises to alter the outlook of people all over the world. Although the issue of toilet access might seem trivial or foolish, it is actually central to the public controversy, since it constitutes one of the essential functions and rights of all human beings. One way of oppressing people worldwide is to deny them a comfortable and safe way to relieve themselves. During the era of segregation in the United States, "Whites Only" restrooms were ubiquitous in the South. In many countries around the globe, women and other subjugated groups are not provided with public restrooms or workplace facilities, a situation that causes health problems, leaves people vulnerable to rape or attack, and thus discourages them from leaving the domestic sphere and participating fully in society. In a similar pattern of systemic oppression, agricultural and manual laborers are often denied the dignity of proper facilities and break time to relieve themselves. Many of the films discussed in *Transgender Cinema* contain pivotal scenes depicting how the right to use toilets is a critical issue for trans people. Among filmmakers, artists, and scholars in the LGBTQ community, different ideologies and judgments surface; even those in broad agreement with the goals of trans filmmakers disagree on the best methods for transforming the world as we know it. *Transgender Cinema* tells the story of this ongoing evolution.

The first step in scholarly work involves defining the subject and scope of study, and trans cinema provides one of the trickiest categories to pin down with precision. Various groups have a different stake in the matter, while film scholars work to survey the field, identify commonly used terms and definitions, and delineate the origins and progression of films that portray trans identity. This discussion will use the terms "transgender" or "trans" for individuals whose gender identity or identification is not the sex of male or female assigned at birth. The manifestations may include cross-dressing (sometimes referred to as transvestite dress), drag, and other intersexed or non-conforming gender categories, gender queer behavior, or identification. "Cisgender" refers to people whose gender identity conforms to the sex assigned at birth. Occasionally, this text may quote negative terms in the context of individuals speaking to describe themselves, but these are employed only for purposes of analysis and understanding, never to convey derogatory judgments or to perpetuate stereotypes or condone biased language.

Because one inherent feature of trans experience is the blurring of boundaries, the task of delineating categories of sex and gender presents an almost paradoxical challenge. Setting limitations or rigid definitions may distort rather than reveal the lived experiences of transgender people. This book covers primarily English-language films, but it also provides a sampling of the rich body of international terms and transgender films, which could easily fill another volume. It can be astonishing to discover the complexity and variety of national and cultural approaches and attitudes toward transsexual identity. For instance, non-English terms for gender variation coming from non-Western cultures include the following, all of which designate slightly different nuances: Hijra, Aka-va'ine, Bakla, Bissu, Calabai, Fa'afafine, Fakaleiti, Kathoey, Khanith, Koekchuch, Māhū, Maknyah, Mukhannathun, Muxe, Takatāpui, Travesti, and Two-Spirit Winkte.

Writing about films of the transgender community involves a specific vocabulary, from pronoun usage to medical descriptions. Agreeing on common terms can be a challenge, because language is constantly evolving. "Cis-" is a Latin prefix meaning "on the same side as" and is therefore an antonym of "trans" (Morrison 25).

"Cisgender" is used to describe people who are not transgender. The American Psychiatric Association uses "gender dysphoria" to designate a condition in which the sex assigned at birth does not match a person's gender identity. Many transgender advocates see this medical diagnosis as an important and necessary distinction, in order to assure that health insurance covers treatments for transgender people.

"Gender expression" is any external manifestation of gender, such as names, pronouns, clothing, haircut, behavior, voice, or body characteristics. Most transgender people try to align gender expression with gender identity, rather than with the sex assigned at birth. "Gender identity" is an internal and firmly held sense of one's gender, and for transgender individuals, this does not match the gender assigned at birth. "Gender nonconforming" describes people whose gender expression differs from socially expected masculine and feminine conventions. "Genderqueer" is used to describe people whose gender identity and/or gender expression do not conform to male and female categories.

The Associated Press style guide recommends referring to individuals by their preferred gendered pronouns, asking for a preference, or using pronouns that conform with an individual's gender expression. Major publications follow this rule, but some writers use gender-neutral pronouns such as singular "they" or terms such as "ze" or "xe." The *Washington Post* announced acceptance of the singular "they," and the *New York Times* allowed the honorific "Mx." The editor Philip Corbett explains that no set rules on gender-neutral terms exist yet, and the paper has avoided using "nontraditional" pronouns. In contrast, *BuzzFeed* uses any preferred pronoun, possibly with a short gloss.

Other terms have acronyms or abbreviations that serve as a convenient shorthand. "Sex reassignment surgery" (SRS; sometimes called "gender reassignment" or "gender affirming" surgery) describes surgical interventions, which not all transgender people can afford or choose to undergo. "Transgender," often abbreviated as "trans," is a general term for those whose gender identity and/or gender expression differs from "what is typically associated with the sex they were assigned at birth." A transgender man or female to male (FTM) is considered female at birth but identifies and lives as a man. A transgender woman or male to female (MTF) is considered male at birth but identifies and lives as a female. "Transition" describes a complex process of altering one's birth sex—occurring over a long time period from six months to a year or several years—usually including medical and legal steps, using a different name and personal pronouns, dressing differently, taking hormones, and perhaps having surgery.

In addition to seeking diversity and global variety, another challenge in choosing examples from Western and other cultures is to select works that represent some combination of films that are influential, artistically interesting, varied, representative, and reasonably available. These choices necessitate some background, particularly for examples from countries that vary widely in their terminology and cultural practices. For example, Iran's rich national cinema is the result of practically total censorship of films from outside the country. Homosexual themes or characters are strictly forbidden, yet transgender characters and individuals in the society are more readily accepted and accommodated in some ways than they are in many Western nations. Because of some people's belief that Koranic teachings distinguish between body and soul, transgender individuals and their desired outcomes are viewed by many Iranians as medical issues, rather than ethical dilemmas. The nation has a sophisticated, booming investment in transgender surgeries, support groups, and workshops for transgender individuals and their families. Filmmakers have responded with their artistic depictions of transgender characters, one of the most notable being Negar Azarbayjani's *Facing Mirrors*

(Iran, *Aynehaye Rooberoo*, 2011). This film tells the story of Rana, a poor woman who drives a cab, and her wealthy transgender passenger, Adineh (Eddie), who is on the way to have reassignment surgery. In the course of their journey, Adineh's mission is revealed, and the audience learns about the conflicting views of these two very different individuals. One caveat in considering Iranian examples of films and cultural practices is concern over reports that transgender surgeries are sometimes forced on gay or lesbian individuals in order to avoid social stigma or family shame in a religious culture that strictly outlaws homosexual relationships and activities.

In the Philippines, similarly strict standards apply in regard to transgender behavior and identity. Although there is no broadly accepted or socially recognized category for gay men or women, there does exist a slightly more tolerant attitude toward the expression of effeminate and cross-dressing boys, particularly in pre-adolescent and early teen years. An example of a Filipino transgender character is evident in the adolescent character Maxi in Auraeus Solito's *The Blossoming of Maximo Oliveros* (2005). Before beginning on the odyssey of contemporary films, which will constitute the bulk of this volume, it is enlightening and valuable to put such works in a historical context, seeking out the roots of transgender cinema and the groundbreaking examples that continue to inspire interest and admiration from transsexuals, the LGBTQ community, and the larger culture of the early twenty-first century.

A final challenge is to get some sense of the big picture around the globe and even within American media. A neglected aspect of analyzing large patterns in trans cinema is consideration of major differences between films about trans men and those about trans women. Wikipedia's "List of Transgender Characters in Film and Television" includes sixteen titles for trans men, sixty-two for trans women, and one film with both male and female characters. This listing, of course, is a communally developed public compilation that omits quite a few titles, but it is interesting to note the imbalance between the number of films depicting trans men or male trans characters and the number of films including trans women individuals or characters. Another fascinating distinction is the contrast between film and television portrayals, among the seventy-six television episodes featuring a transgender character captured in this same listing. Although films generally lead the field, television seems to have overtaken film in sheer quantity and variety of depictions in recent years. A few notable examples represent revolutionary change, for example, in the *Dark Angel* television series, when Normal dates Louise (Jessica Crockett) and discovers that she is transgender. The fact that Crockett is a trans woman playing a trans character was a first for American television. Although Normal decides that he likes her and that her sexual past does not matter, in a final twist, he then learns that she is also a lesbian.

Outside of American cultures, one finds more openness in understanding and cultural practices that affect transgender individuals. Noting how Pacific and Native American civilizations—among many other cultures—had terms for various trans community members long before humans had media technology to represent them or medical technology to fully accomplish physical transitions, this work begins the first chapter by discussing how trans individuals have been or continue to be persecuted or ignored in some cultures, while other societies view trans members in varying degrees as valued contributors to the life of the community. Most early film depictions of twentieth-century trans characters are a far cry from such promising representations, but every decade since the beginning of film has produced works that offer complex narratives and characters who escape restrictions and expand or breach standard gender boundaries. Even tragic stories hold the seeds of triumph. With an emphasis on analysis rather than evaluation, this work will focus on films that represent a common category of depictions or typify a standard pattern, along with those that constitute

singular creative contributions to our evolving understanding of what it means and how it feels to be transgender. The organization of this volume makes a nod to
early examples in the canon of transgender representation
and then moves to the major stages of development, with
turning points beginning in the 1960s, around the end of
the twentieth century, and with the new millennium. It
is useful to survey common patterns, stereotypes, and
archetypal depictions of transgender characters from the
origins of film to the later twentieth century, looking at
representative, canonical, and sometimes negative depictions of transgender figures.

Chapter 1, "Trans Tropes," discusses figures such as
Charlie Chaplin in silent and early films, western serial
queens, androgynous femmes fatales such as Marlene
Dietrich in *Morocco* (1930), Greta Garbo in *Queen Christina* (1933), and others in *Glen or Glenda* (1953), *Psycho*
(1960), *Some Like It Hot* (1959), *Myra Breckinridge* (1970),
and *La Cage aux Folles* (1978). The chapter looks at early
imitations of transgender figures, noting the avant-garde
trans stars featured in Andy Warhol's and John Waters's
work, and the problematic nature of portraying trans
people as psychotics and criminals, as depicted in *Psycho*
(1960), *The Tenant* (1976), and *Silence of the Lambs* (1991).
It analyzes the double-edged sword of powerful yet car-
toonish comic trans figures, as represented in *Some Like It*

Hot (1959), *I Was a Male War Bride* (1949), *Tootsie* (1982), *La Cage aux Folles* (1978), *Myra Breckinridge* (1970), and *The Rocky Horror Picture Show* (1975). Finally, it considers other classic precursors to authentic and complex portrayals emerging in recent decades. Most films of earlier eras depict more male-to-female trans characters than female-to-male characters, the vast majority of which are played by cisgender or gender-conforming actors. These depictions—while riddled with and often creating clichés about transgender people—offered more than a catalog of what not to do. Some also broke ground and offered visibility to a neglected demographic, and such films continue to provide not just laughs or groans; they offer a sense of presence and inclusion over time. They may also offer inspiration, possible encouragement, and a sense of participation, visibility, and influence in the larger society.

Chapter 1 also looks at exceptional works—often international and relatively independent films of recent decades—that have made singular contributions by aiming for creative and original approaches to transgender lives and issues. For example, Sally Potter's adaptation of Virginia Woolf's *Orlando* has Tilda Swinton playing both male and female versions of the eponymous protagonist. In the same year, Neil Jordan's *The Crying Game* (1992) shatters convention by revealing a penis onscreen and having the heterosexual lead, Fergus (Stephen Rea),

continue his intense and caring relationship with the Dil
(Jaye Davidson), the leading trans woman, even after
he sees her male sexual equipment. With pressure from
enlightened audiences and a growing awareness of the
need for greater authenticity, Pedro Almodóvar casts
trans and cisgender actors to play both kinds of characters
in *All about My Mother* (1999), challenging strict barriers
and distinctions in gender and sexual identity.

Chapter 2, "Breaking Boundaries in the New Millennium," analyzes developments in the early twenty-first
century, focusing on various controversies surrounding
groundbreaking films, television series, nonconforming
celebrities, and cultural icons. Meanwhile, international
cinema produced a number of complex and sophisticated
works depicting transgender lives, through powerful
documentaries such as *Southern Comfort* (2001), *Georgie
Girl* (2002), and *Girl Inside* (2009) and such fictional narratives as *The Blossoming of Maximo Oliveros* (2005) and
Tomboy (2011).

Chapter 3, "New Platforms and New Voices," considers
how the new millennium eventually found its legs, with
trans characters and actors emerging in even greater variety and numbers in documentaries, popular films, and
television series. Whereas Felicity Huffman's attempt
to play a transitioning male to female in *TransAmerica*
(2005) bombed, and the cisgender Elle Fanning was

widely panned for her reenactment of a transitioning boy in *Three Generations* (2015), Jill Soloway created a popular hit with Jeffrey Tambor as a transitioning mom in *Transparent* (2014), an Amazon web-based series. In addition to these works, CBS and NBC human-interest pieces featured a variety of transgender figures, including Chaz Bono and the former Olympic pentathlon winner Caitlin Jenner. Audiences were not drawn solely to fictional or celebrity lives, however. The chapter considers how depictions of real lives in serious documentaries, television movies, and online transgender media communities altered the public conversation about gender identity. All of these controversial trans figures place consumers, characters, and actors in an artificial context outside of—yet deeply connected to—the lived experience depicted in artistic, popular, documentary, and intertextual trans narratives.

1

TRANS TROPES

Transgender people have always existed, but societies have had a variety of ways to depict and express the experience of these individuals throughout the ages. Developments in film and medicine at the beginning of the twentieth century created new modes of expressing, altering, and thinking about gender identity. Before medical science began its attempts to alter sex characteristics, films depicted and documented examples of transgender people. Although these depictions tended to fall into two categories—comic or pathological—there were exceptions to these broad classifications. Charlie Chaplin often took advantage of his large dark eyes, playing female characters who sometimes looked surprisingly feminine, particularly in *The Masquerader* (1914), *A Busy Day* (1914), and *A Woman* (1915). Some sort of pandemonium and disruption usually ensued with the presence of a female Chaplin, but the actor often blended elements of humanity and seriousness into his comedy, pointing to social foibles and inequalities.

People have commented throughout the decades on the androgynous quality of Chaplin. In fact, in a You-Tube video arguing that Charlie Chaplin was actually a woman, the narrator takes a bioanthropological approach to the physical features of Chaplin, attempting to prove by physical analysis that he was actually a "she" (Humanity). In the video's opening, the narrator notes a coincidental correlation that the last castrato (person castrated in order to sing as a soprano and not have masculine sex characteristics) died in 1890, a year after Chaplin was born. The speaker in this video offers photographs of Chaplin and analyzes the physical details characteristic of masculine physiognomy. He notes the absence of an Adam's apple or brow ridge and points to the bulbous forehead and narrow shoulders in relation to the hips, all common characteristics of female anatomy. One could make counterarguments, for example, the fact that when Chaplin speaks for the first time on film, playing a Hitler look-alike in *The Great Dictator* (1940), his voice does not sound like a woman's voice. In addition, his daughter, Geraldine Chaplin, bears a strong resemblance to Charlie, as do several others of the eleven children he claimed to have fathered from three different wives. Regardless of whether one accepts far-fetched claims about Chaplin's hidden female gender, it must be acknowledged that Chaplin's cross-dressing performances and persona constitute a memorable facet of this legendary artist's androgynous persona, one that helped open the door for transgender presence in film from its beginnings.

After the serial queens of early western films, such as Pearl White, Helen Holmes, Ann Little, Ruth Roland, and Marin Sais, pushed gender boundaries by doing their own stunts and wearing masculine cowboy gear, two European stars arrived on American screens, standing out as androgynous icons. Greta Garbo was famous for her sultry voice and iconic role in *Queen Christina* (1933), playing a woman who was raised as a man, for all practical purposes: "In keeping with her upbringing, she has a manservant who helps her on with her pants and boots and combs her hair as she reads Molière. When her father advises her that she will die an old maid, she quickly replies, 'I shall die a bachelor!'" (Bell-Metereau 75). During the first third of the film, she maintains this masculine persona, through clothing, voice, and gesture, but we see her transform into a more traditionally staid feminine role as she falls in love with the Spanish ambassador, Antonio (John Gilbert): "It is in repose, not in movement, that she first reveals to Antonio that obvious outline of her breast beneath her thin shirt. She is still dressed as a man, but there is gentleness of expression—her head lowered and her body angled at three-quarters profile, one knee demurely bent in, in the classic pose combining feminine modesty and seductiveness" (Bell-Metereau 75–76). Enthralled by love, Christina succumbs to tradition and becomes more passive, exhibiting more emotion and fragility, but by the end of the film, with the loss of her male lover, she regains toughness and returns to the stoic and gender-nonconforming persona exhibited in the film's opening.

Marlene Dietrich presents one of the most indelible images of the classic androgynous femme fatale, but some film scholars argue that Josef von Sternberg played Svengali to Dietrich's androgynous persona. It was reported that Sternberg once said, "I am Miss Dietrich—Miss Dietrich is me" (Bell-Metereau 104). Sternberg's fascination with cross-dressing may have come from his jobs as a youth in a millinery shop and lace house in New York: "One can easily imagine the impressionable fifteen-year-old immigrant losing himself in reveries as he would clean the shop, filled with lace, feathers, artificial flowers and fruit, hat forms, manikins, and the lingering perfume of the day's customers. These erotically charged visual experiences would become the building blocks of Sternberg's film world" (Bell-Metereau 105). Practically every Sternberg film with Dietrich features her powerful frame draped in masculine clothing and helpless men adorned in bits of female finery, as they are enthralled by her powerful beauty.

Although Laura Mulvey's work develops the idea that the typical filmic masculine gaze inevitably creates a relationship of male domination, I see a different paradigm, wherein "voyeurism is central to Sternberg's concept of man's relationship to woman, for in his schema, to gaze is to worship. Man's desire to look at woman does not, as many feminists claim, make her a mere object; rather, in Sternberg's world, it gives her almost unlimited power" (Bell-Metereau 105). Andrew Sarris argues in a similar vein that for Sternberg, "the Girl will possess a mystical authority over the life of the Boy, and it is this authority which marks Sternberg's attitude toward women long before the debut of Marlene Dietrich" (39).

Dietrich went on to play other androgynous roles without Sternberg, and "after his 1935 farewell film with Dietrich (*The Devil Is a Woman*), the director continued to create films of sexual reversal, if not celebrating androgyny, exploring it with all the thoroughness and morbid curiosity of a child examining a squashed bug" (Bell-Metereau 106). In his final film, *The Saga of Anatahan* (1953), Sternberg incorporates the idea of organic unity in male and female relationships: twelve Japanese sailors chant to the singular "Queen Bee," among them, "'You and I, like an egg—you, egg yellow, I egg white—I embrace you!' This chant indicates the symbiotic aspect of the combination as well as the centrality of the female figure, the yolk that consumes the white as it grows" (Bell-Metereau 106–7).

With World War II, films in the United States grappled with changing gender roles, and Cary Grant dresses as an extremely uncomfortable WAC to follow his new bride to America in Howard Hawks's *I Was a Male War Bride* (1949). This agonized representation of sex-role reversal contrasts with Billy Wilder's groundbreaking *Some Like It Hot* (1959), appearing only a decade later. Jack Lemmon plays a cross-dressing member of an all-girl band, Daphne, who engages in a romance with a millionaire named Osgood (Joe E. Brown). The film is famous for its ending, in which Daphne confesses that he cannot marry Osgood because he is actually a man, to which Osgood replies, "Nobody's perfect." Although this is a comedy, filled with exaggeration and caricature, it is tantalizing in its open ending, hinting at the possibility of gender-nonconforming marriage. The end of the 1950s paved the way for a number of portrayals of psychotic transgender characters, the most infamous being the schizophrenic Norman Bates (Anthony Perkins) in Alfred Hitchcock's *Psycho* (1959). Although the film depicts a monstrous character, he is portrayed with such subtlety and charm by Perkins that he was never able to escape the persona created by the film.

While Hitchcock's *Psycho* endures in the pantheon of classic cross-dressing psychological thrillers, William Castle's *Homicidal* (1961) stands out as a somewhat neglected homage to *Psycho*, with many of its psychological subtleties unrecognized. As David Sanjek observes, Castle's most famous film (perhaps aside from cheesy cult favorite *The Tingler* [1959]) was *Homicidal*, precisely because it offers hints at a backstory of the abuse and torture that produces the character of Warren/Emily, a psychopathic transvestite: few trash films, whether produced within or outside the Hollywood system, treat their characters, and particularly their "monsters," as anything more or less than cardboard figures with little substance other than the function they serve in a rudimentary narrative. Even less frequently do trash filmmakers induce sympathy or pity for their characters. *Homicidal* is an exception to the rule and the only film that Castle produced that not only scares one's pants off but also brings a tear to one's eye for the fate of the "monster" (Sanjek 248). In spite of such praise, Sanjek also argues that, unlike *Psycho*, Castle's *Homicidal* lacks "a sense of the desolate core of American life" (260). The film's allusions to sex-change procedures in Denmark suggest the possibility of surgical sex alteration, but the director leaves the question open-ended. Ultimately, Castle is not necessarily progressive in his depiction of such operations, but the mere mention of the Scandinavian treatment was daring. The film's conclusion follows Robin Wood's claim that horror films offer a binary of the repressed other in the monster, viewing the project of horror films as "the struggle for recognition of all that our civilization *represses* or *oppresses*, . . . an object of horror, a matter for terror," with a " 'happy ending' (when it exists) typically signifying the restoration of repression" (201). Audiences felt sympathy and sometimes covert admiration for the characters in both *Psycho* and *Homicidal*, a pattern later repeated in Anthony Hopkins's description of a cannibalistic figure who wants to literally crawl inside his mother's skin in *Silence of the Lambs*.

During the 1960s and 1970s, avant-garde artists had their share of raucous and X-rated fun with gender, beginning with Jack Smith's underground experimental film *Flaming Creatures* (1963). Opening at New York's Bleecker Street Cinema, the film tested obscenity laws, with a number of venues avoiding exhibition, while one suffered a police raid for showing the short film. In 1964, police stormed into a screening by Ken Jacobs, Jonas Mekas, and Florence Karpf, seizing the print and charging violation of the obscenity law in New York. This action prompted Susan Sontag and Mekas to flood the media with statements and essays arguing for freedom of expression and the artistic merits of the film, thus ironically catapulting the film to notoriety and cult status far beyond anyone's expectations. Smith's work appears to be randomly structured, opening with hand-lettered title and cast pages, a fuzzy shot of a long-haired woman, random shots of a flaccid penis, and a hilarious advertisement for lipstick, jumping to a graphic orgy scene and finally concluding with an orgasmic earthquake. Cloudy black-and-white visuals, scratchy melodramatic orchestral accompaniment, and references to Ali Baba recall the era of early film. In a campy ad scene, actors in drag do a fake commercial that asks the question, "Is there lipstick that doesn't come off when you suck cocks?"

The controversy over this film continued for years, with critical reception ranging from complete dismissal of the artistic merit to Sontag declaring the film a "rare modern work of art: it is about joy and innocence" (229). Groups that encountered interference with exhibition of the film included the University of New Mexico, the University of Texas, the University of Michigan, and the University of Notre Dame, which erupted in the school's first violent conflict between students and police in 1969. The state supreme court of New York reversed the conviction of the exhibitors, and eventually in the 1990s, major institutions began exhibiting the work. Fifty years after the original arrests, the prosecutor issued an apology to Mekas for his misguided attitudes toward censorship.

Even more famous but much less controversial for including transgender actors, Andy Warhol cultivated Holly Woodlawn and Candy Darling, who starred in the art films *Flesh* (1968), *Trash* (1970), and *Women in Revolt* (1972). Woodlawn, a Puerto Rican actress, was also known as Holly in Lou Reed's "Walk on the Wild Side." Reaching larger audiences, quirky films such as *Myra Breckenridge* (1970) and *La Cage aux Folles* (1978) drew art-house viewers. Jim Sharman's *The Rocky Horror Picture Show* (1975), based on the successful musical, built a cult following for repeat midnight showings, in which the audience came in drag, singing, dancing, reciting lines, and playing with props such as newspaper hats and water pistols. Sydney Pollack's *Tootsie* (1982), aimed at popular audiences, garnered Academy Awards and prompted the lead actor, Dustin Hoffman, to admit that—like many women—he also wanted to be beautiful. Although these films all reflect growing shifts in public attitudes, it is not until the 1990s that real changes occurred in a large number of serious mainstream films.

If films of the 1960s, 1970s, and 1980s generally presented shallow or distorted portrayals of transgender characters as comic, psychotic, scary, or pitiful, the 1990s witnessed an explosion of more nuanced portraits. The decade offers a pivotal transformation in the depiction of transgender protagonists and LGBTQ pioneers. Some of these pioneers have popped up in unexpected places, including the late twentieth-century Harlem drag scene, the early twentieth-century literary scene, and the arrival in the West from Japan of the form of anime. Three outstanding examples reflect these trends: Jennifer Livingston's *Paris Is Burning* (1991), Sally Potter's *Orlando*, and the anime series *Sailor Moon* (1992).

Livingston broke new ground in the documentary *Paris Is Burning*, but not without controversy. The director spent seven years getting to know the African American and Hispanic participants in drag balls in Harlem and understanding the social structure surrounding these entertainments. The expected drag categories include gender-bending clothing, but Livingston also documents expanded concepts of drag with categories such as "Town and Country," "Military," or "Executive." Participants' discussions of these categories reflect a sophisticated understanding of the ways in which we all are "in drag" in one form or another, presenting an identity through clothing and body modifications. Most of the contestants belong to a "House," such as LaBeija, Extravaganza, or Pendavis, run by a "legendary" head of the household, many of whom call themselves "mothers" to their younger followers. Livingston's film offers an intimate glimpse into a world where participants open up to her and share their dreams and fears.

With the success of *Paris Is Burning*, Livingston was accused of various forms of exploitation. bell hooks argues that "what viewers witness is not black men longing to impersonate or even to become like 'real' black women but their obsession with an idealized fetishized vision of femininity that is white" (148). Livingston was also accused of exploiting and co-opting black experience. She found herself in a bind, with regard to compensating her subjects: a journalistic ethic would forbid her from paying interviewees, while a humanitarian ethic would dictate compensation to people who have low or no income. She was sued for $40 million by one participant, although the film only grossed $3,779,620 in the United States. The subjects dropped their claims when attorneys showed signed releases and awarded about $55,000 to thirteen participants (Green).

When the renowned novelist Virginia Woolf wrote *Orlando*—the fanciful tale of an Elizabethan aristocrat who miraculously survives for several centuries and transforms into a woman along the way—she had no idea that the central character would become a transgender movie icon. Woolf was suspicious of cinema, and as one of the first to write about film adaptations of literature, she claimed that cinema "largely subsists upon the body of its unfortunate victim" (350). The director Sally Potter recognized the rich cinematic possibilities for Woolf's novel and cast a lanky Tilda Swinton as the ambiguously gendered lead in *Orlando*, a 1992 art-house film that continues to delight lovers of Woolf, androgyny, and quirky satires about English literature and society. Swinton had stage experience with trans roles, playing a woman who impersonates a male in Manfred Karge's 1988 translation of Bertolt Brecht's *Man to Man*, a World War II piece about a woman who disguises herself as a man in order to take over her dead husband's job. Swinton also played Mozart in the stage production of Aleksandr Pushkin's *Mozart and Salieri*. Slim, square-shouldered, fair-haired, and almost six feet tall, Swinton was a natural fit for the role of Orlando. Like the fictional character, Swinton studied English literature and came from an ancient aristocratic family.

The scholars Sara Villa and Sharon Ouditt observe significant connections between the novel and Potter's film adaptation. In spite of Woolf's use of the negative vampire image for film adaptation, she makes self-conscious use of photographs, cinematic devices, and imagery in her novel, as if foretelling the decline of the novel as the dominant narrative genre. Some transgender critics claim that Woolf's original novel has no legitimate place in the canon of trans literature, because it presents a figure who has no previous desire to change genders, goes through no transition phase, and seems relatively untroubled in her posttransition life as a female. Chris Coffman argues, however, that despite these differences, contemporary readers should "read Orlando's interrogation of desire, gender, and embodiment as productively aligned with contemporary feminist and transgender politics."

The background to the novel is a relevant footnote to the film, starting with a dedication to Woolf's beloved Vita Sackville-West. This aristocratic connection sets the stage for an allegory of the declining fortunes of the Sackville-West family and of many other noble families in England. Woolf critiques the precarious position of female heirs in the British primogeniture system of inherited titles and property, passed exclusively through male lines. On a more powerful and personal level, people familiar with Woolf's intimate relationship with Sackville-West immediately recognized a resemblance between Orlando and Woolf's friend, whose son, Nigel Nicolson, calls the novel "the longest and most charming love letter in literature, in which [Woolf] explores Vita, weaves her in and out of the centuries, tosses her from one sex to the other, plays with her, dresses her in furs, lace and emeralds, teases her, flirts with her, drops a veil of mist around her" (203). If the novel was Woolf's love letter to Sackville-West, Sally Potter's film adaptation was her love letter to Woolf and her powerful trans character. Updating the narrative, Potter still uses self-conscious shots in which Swinton gazes directly into the camera, not unlike Woolf's frequent direct addresses to her readers.

The recurring criticism of films depicting LGBTQ characters with the use of straight or nontransgender actors goes back to Stephan Elliott's *The Adventures of Priscilla, Queen of the Desert* (1994), which features Terrence Stamp playing an aging drag queen on tour in Australia. The film enjoyed widespread international popularity on its release and has since become a lasting cult classic. Although it may be argued that Stamp has no way of relating authentically to the character, this assumes that a straight or nontransgender actor has no sense of vanity or desire to be beautiful. The strategies used in this film demonstrate how identification may be achieved through a combination of intelligent direction and technical effects.

Given that movies convey a large amount of information in an incredibly condensed space, lighting keys (like genres or formulaic narratives) provide the audience with a visual guide for how to read a film. Cinematographers also utilize these keys to produce unconventional effects and unexpected results. For instance, the cinematographer Brian Breheny shot Stamp (playing the cross-dresser Ralph/Bernadette Bassenger) with hard light that accentuated the actor's wrinkles. Meanwhile, off the set, the crew had Stamp's dressing table lit with soft flattering light that diminishes lines and shadows on the actor's aging face. The actor was therefore able to imagine himself as a beautiful woman, created by the magic of soft, even lighting, which visually eliminates or minimizes shadows, wrinkles, and sagging skin. Elliott did not let Stamp view the dailies, so the actor had no idea how old and haggard he looked in the actual footage. When Stamp saw the final product, shot with hard lighting and harsh, direct sunlight, the actor reportedly cried. The camp icon Bette Davis supposedly had the same reaction to her appearance in the story of an aging child star when she saw herself at the premiere of *Whatever Happened to Baby Jane?* (1962). Even ordinary nonperformers want to look as good as possible, but many actors—whose egos and livelihoods depend on their looks—are especially invested in appearing to be beautiful, regardless of gender or age. Skilled directors and lighting artists can exploit this tendency and use technical sleight of hand for dramatic effect, creating a compelling performance of gender by playing on an actor's vanity.

Priscilla, Queen of the Desert does not portray a trans woman, per se, but this film opened up the door and has continued to inspire some members of the LGBTQ community for decades. However, as Glenn Dunks observes, "For all the success that *The Adventures of Priscilla, Queen of the Desert* has found, it was not a harbinger of things immediately to come," noting the disconnect between filmic representation and the society at large: "In the decade after the year 2000, fiction features with queer themes dropped off substantially. . . . One might have expected Australian filmmakers to more accurately represent queer culture in light of changes in societal attitudes towards the LGBTQIA community" (31). It is possible to account for this decline in light of the events of 9/11, which moved media attention in the direction of more traditional gender roles, but another avenue is to look at the emergence of transgender figures in mainstream television. While television and film have always exerted mutual influence, with television generally trailing behind in its daring and innovation, the decline of the film industry has been accompanied by an expansion and conglomeration of media platforms, particularly with the rise of the internet. Cable television once supplanted traditional theaters in popularity and influence, but more recently web-based venues and binge watching of series such as *Orange Is the New Black* have sidelined traditional television platforms. With the rise and fall of various outlets, fortunes are made, but these modes of viewing do not simply disappear. Rather, they evolve and adapt as commercial rewards shift like quicksand.

Translation and distribution have an outsized influence in limiting Western access to global images of transgender figures. In 1992, the animated (anime) *Sailor Moon* series caught on like wildfire among a generation of girls, as part of a massive increase in consumption of Japanese cultural and commercial products. N'Donna Russell calls the sexually progressive series—including gay males, non-binary males and females, and a lesbian duo—"one of the most popular anime series of all time." What is notable is how the series was altered in its English translation and the episodes available for Western (primarily American) consumption. In the dubbed version, Sailor Neptune and Sailor Uranus are changed from lesbian characters to cousins, which creates some peculiar incestuous overtones for certain scenes.

Although many Americans consider themselves to be members of the most liberated and advanced culture in the world, the case of *Sailor Moon*, created by Naoko Takeuchi and released in 1991 as a serial comic (manga), provides a perfect example of the suppression of content in order to support a heteronormative and constrictive social standard. Even the translation of the Japanese title, "Bishoujo Senshi Sailor Moon," which means "pretty soldier Sailor Moon," becomes the less sexually ambiguous "Sailor Moon," and in translation, characters are called the diminutive "sailor scouts" rather than "Sailor Soldiers" ("Are Phobos"), making them sound like Girl Scouts on adventures, not female soldiers saving the world.

In each episode, the pretty protagonist, the spoiled yet loyal Sailor Moon (Usagi or Serena in English), leads four friends to defeat monsters and save the day. Sara Roncero-Menendez explains reception of the series: "Anime fans will be able to enjoy the show for the same reasons I did; because the women in it felt like real people, people I knew and who I wanted to be like." Tokyopop reported selling over a million of the English print editions of the manga since 2001 ("Sailor Moon Graphic"). *Sailor Moon* combines the best of empowering or androgynous qualities with the Japanese concept of *shojo*, or girlishness: "In Japan, the cultural significance of magical girls stems from their themes of empowerment and independence while retaining traditionally feminine traits" (Russell). The most obvious queer couple, Uranus and Neptune, appear in the final three seasons in a relationship that is depicted as normal, paralleling the heterosexual relationship of Sailor Moon and Tuxedo Mask, the other main couple of the series. It is presented as a given, while the romance of Moon and Tuxedo Mask grows over time. Even the depiction of the heterosexual couple challenges gender categories through cross-dressing: "An analysis of Sailor Uranus, also known as *Haruka Tenoh*, can show a resistance to the gender binary that has been typically enforced by children's media. Haruka in her civilian clothes dresses in varying styles, and is drawn as taller than the other Soldiers. She chooses when to present as male and as female through her use of the male school uniform; this subversion of the school uniform as a figure of rigid gender binary upsets the way we view young high school girls" (Vanaerde 12).

The new characters of Uranus and Neptune in *Sailor Moon* were not the first queer representation; the villains Zoisite and Kunzite (Malachite in the dubbed version) were coded as gay, but in translation, their sexes and relationship were altered for American consumption. In the Japanese version, Zoisite was a blond, long-haired, androgynous male in a homosexual relationship with Kunzite, but for U.S. consumption, his character's gender was altered by using the voice dub of Kirsten Bishop ("Sailor Moon TV"), thus eliminating the controversial gay couple. As Roncero-Menendez suggests, the confusing translation and censorship or alteration of gay or lesbian content betray the intent of the original series. Audiences in the United States were not allowed to see trans-appearing characters, such as the young people in the musical trio Sailor Star Lights. These characters are in a male boy band during the day, but they become female Sailor Soldiers at night. According to Sigourney Vanaerde, the "Star Lights offered an example of trans visibility (problematic though it may be), which made this part of the series completely unacceptable for dubbing according to the Western translators for Toei; it wasn't even aired in the U.S. due to the trans-antagonist views of the production company" (13). This may be seen as a temporary setback for fans, given the growing audience for transgender media of all kinds, along with the willingness of companies to make money on viewer demand.

Alain Berliner's *Ma Vie en Rose* (1997) was Belgium's submission for the 1997 Best Foreign Language Film Oscar, but it did not receive a nomination from the Motion Picture Arts Academy (MPAA). The screenplay for the film is the work of Chris vander Stappen, whom Roger Ebert identifies as "herself a tomboy who got a lot of heat as a child" (*"Ma Vie"*). It also received an R rating from the MPAA, despite the film's mild language and lack of nudity, violence, or sexually suggestive scenes. It did win the 1997 Golden Globe Award for Best Foreign Language Film and the GLAAD Media Award for outstanding film, limited release, however. The film challenges gender categories by presenting the story of Ludovic, who is convinced that he is really a girl who has mysteriously failed to receive one of the required X chromosomes. When he persists in dressing like a girl, his school eventually receives a petition from parents requesting his expulsion. The entire neighborhood shuns the family; eventually the father loses his job, and they are forced to move to another city, where he finds work. The film does not directly address issues of homosexuality or sexuality in general. Nonetheless, a website that questioned why this mild film had an R rating received an alert from CyberPatrol, software designed for parents to block web content from children (Peacefire). The website (www.thirdtablet.com/WhyIsMaVieEnRoseRatedR) was then blocked.

The film presents parents who are desperate to "solve the problem" of their child's persistent sense that she is really a girl. The grandmother is sympathetic, suggesting that they simply play along until Ludo outgrows this experimental phase. They consider this option, but their child does not seem to become bored with being a girl. As more and more of their neighbors ostracize them, the mother and father grow increasingly impatient with Ludo's insistence on dressing like a girl. The community has a variety of responses, including one scene in which everyone accepts the ludic aspects of the situation and start dancing and enjoying the freedom offered by this unconventional child. Eventually, though, the mother becomes enraged when all of her attempts at a "cure" fail. She brutally beats Ludo, taking her frustration out on her child and collapsing in tears. At this point, the fanciful fairy godmother of Ludo arrives and rescues her.

Eleven-year-old Georges du Fresne plays the role of Ludo with an innocence and seriousness that fits the character's predicament. Ludo wants desperately to marry the boy next door, as any little girl might imagine doing. Although the parents are alarmed, Ludo's conception of this plan is without sexual overtones. When Ludo's world becomes too much to bear, he escapes to an imaginary realm based on a television star named Pam, who wears pink princess outfits, has a boyfriend named Ken (just like Barbie's boyfriend, one might add), and flits around solving problems with a magic wand. Ludo's other escape is his relationship with his grandmother (a motif that appears several years later in the real-life relationship of Madison, documented in Maya Gallus's 2007 film *Girl Inside*). Ludo becomes an honorary subprincess with similar magical powers, and in the concluding minutes of the film, she escapes to the billboard and the world where Pam makes the rules of the game. The insertion of this fantasy figure lightens the mood of the film, keeps it comic, and softens the parental abuse that might otherwise be too grim a reminder of the challenges that many transgender children face in real life with unaccepting or frustrated parents.

Berliner's film navigates through challenging waters in presenting a transgender child's first same-sex crush. It creates a parody that keeps viewers' sympathies firmly rooted with Ludo, the protagonist. Although there are all the makings for a story of a transgender child, or a child discovering a homosexual relationship, the filmmaker veers away from that challenging content in a sensitive and lighthearted way. It maintains a liminal world that is later echoed in Céline Sciamma's film *Tomboy* (2011), a much more realistic depiction, but one that is just as determined to let its young characters retain their childish innocence. Another factor that these films have in common is the eventual violent response of the parents. Although the parents begin as fairly sympathetic figures, their own anxiety and frustration drive them to treat their children in a brutal and physically violent way. This is particularly shocking for American audiences, who rarely witness onscreen the kind of corporal punishment that occurs all too often in everyday life. Both films also leave the conclusions to the imagination of the audience, and this ambiguity constitutes part of the films' charm.

Roger Ebert points to the real-world issues and injustice behind the lighthearted film *Ma Vie en Rose*: "No one is threatened by a girl who dresses like a boy, but the father's boss is just one of the people who sees red whenever Ludovic turns up in drag. This innocent little boy is made to pay for all the gay phobias, fears and prejudices of the adult world" (*"Ma Vie"*). He goes on to suggest that despite the "sitcom neighborhoods where everyone spends a lot of time out on the lawn or gossiping over the driveways," this story may reflect the challenges of the screenplay author working in a straight world or the experiences of a woman who did not fit expectations for her gender. For all its lighthearted fancy, *Ma Vie en Rose* breaks ground in depicting the experience of a child whose body does not conform with a strong inner sense of identity and the overwhelming desire to outgrow the boyish physical body and grow up to be the princess hidden within.

In the wake of the killing of Matthew Shepard, Kimberley Peirce's powerful 1999 biopic *Boys Don't Cry* shocked audiences and created enormous sympathy for the real-life Brandon Teena (christened Teena Renae Brandon), whose life events inspired the film. Peirce and the screenplay coauthor Andy Beinen researched for four years, using archival footage and lines from Susan Muska and Gréta Olafsdóttir's documentary *The Brandon Teena Story* (1998). Hilary Swank plays Brandon, a transgender man who arrives in Falls City, Nebraska, where he falls in with the ex-cons John Lotter (Peter Sarsgaard) and Tom Nissen (Brendan Sexton III) and falls in love with Lana Tisdel (Chloë Sevigny). Peirce explains why she cast Swank: "I saw someone who not only blurred the gender lines, but who was this beautiful, androgynous person with this cowboy hat and a sock in her pants, who smiled and loved being Brandon" (Basoli). Unaware of Brandon's sexual background, Lana is so smitten with him that she plans to run off to Memphis with him. Even after he is arrested for a prior offense and put in women's prison, she bails him out and accepts his claim that he is a hermaphrodite who has not yet saved enough money for sex-reassignment surgery. When John, Tom, and Lana's friend Lisa discover evidence of Brandon's transgender status, they beat, rape, and eventually murder him. *Boys Don't Cry* drew attention to the plight of transgender individuals, and it also caused controversy among critics and scholars, along with lawsuits and outrage from some of the people whose lives are fictionalized in the film.

Critical response to the film varied widely, with most critics acknowledging the film's powerful message and brilliant acting and direction. Michele Aaron claims that the film emphasizes "the spectacle of transvestism" in its focus on the character's ability to "pass" as male (189). Another viewer sees more nuance, arguing that the film avoids stereotypes, offering a variety of possibilities, including "butch, male, lesbian, transgender, transsexual, and heterosexual . . . and attempting "to subsume the transgressive potential of the gender outlaw within a lesbian framework and narrative" (Driver 185). Julianne Pidduck praises the film for asking the viewer "to experience the rape from the victim's point of view. The film invites political, emotional and corporeal allegiances linked to known and imagined risk, especially for female and/or queer viewers. An allegiance with Brandon's outsider

status aligns the viewer with Brandon's initial exhila-
ration at his transgressive success as a boy, drawing us
through to the film's disturbing finale" (98). Judith Jack
Halberstam praises the film for creating sympathy for
transgender, gay, and lesbian people and views the film
as presenting a narrative in which "the double vision of
the transgender subject gives way to the universal vision
of humanism, the transgender man and his lover become
lesbians and the murder seems instead to be the outcome
of vicious homophobic rage" (*Queer* 91). In a larger discussion of transgender portrayals, Halberstam argues
that the lives of transgender are exposed in media and
film as curiosities and that most objectionable depictions
of transgender lives fall under three project categories:
trivialization, stabilization, and rationalization (*Queer*
54–55). Comedies often trivialize gender issues, and portrayals of transgender people as freaks or psychopaths
contain a project of stabilization, whereas other portrayals with a primarily narrative goal offer rationalization for
the behavior or existence of transgender characters. The
portrayal of real-life and fictional Brandon Teena, both in
news media and film, emphasizes the notion of making
sense of Brandon's life and behavior, placing it under the
category of rationalization.

Other responses to the film's lack of verisimilitude
varied widely, but many of these objections skirted or

ignored the transgender identity at the core of the narrative. Jennifer Devere Brody objects to the film's omission of Philip DeVine, a disabled African American man who was also shot, as an example of racist erasure. Local families' and townspeople's response to Peirce's depiction varied from utter rejection to lawsuits for inaccurate portrayals of persons who lived through the events that took place in 1993. Lana Tisdel claimed that Brandon did not propose to her and that she left him as soon as she learned the truth about his true sexuality, calling the film "the second murder of Brandon Teena" (Farache). Tisdel was primarily offended by the way the film depicted her as low-class and unwilling to prevent a murder, but she settled a lawsuit against Fox Searchlight for an undisclosed figure. Other townspeople disputed the accuracy of the film and its unflattering depiction of the town as well. The fact remains that Teena's death prompted media and locals to try to make sense of the situation, to determine whether Teena was a lesbian, a preoperative transgender person, or a scam artist.

One of the most controversial aspects of *Boys Don't Cry* is its depiction of violence against a transgender person. Peirce "wanted more than anything to depict Brandon so that people would understand and identify with him," but succeeding in this goal also entails viewers identifying with his horrific and violent end (Dannenbaum,

Hodge, and Mayer 137). Although this scene is brutal, the film leads up to this point with a moment of fleeting hope, conveyed through the film's lighting and editing. As Brandon waits for Lana, half of his face is brightly lit, the other in shadow, conveying visually the condition of his hidden conflict. When John and Tom arrive, the air is filled with frantic yells and Lana pleading for Brandon's life. Right before John shoots, Brandon's face appears suffused with hope as he gives a slight smile, gazing into Lana's face when she whispers, "We can still do it," conveying her undying love for him, regardless of biological equipment. At this moment, the sound track goes silent, followed by the blast of a gunshot and a slow-motion shot of Lana wailing, "No!" This editing heightens the shock and emotional impact of the moment, but it simultaneously conveys the presence of a love that transcends physical constraints.

Beginning life as a 1998 successful off-Broadway musical by Mitchell and Stephen Trask, John Cameron Mitchell's *Hedwig and the Angry Inch* (2001) blends fantasy elements with more direct treatment of transgender issues. The film opens with animated representations of round, four-legged, four-armed creatures, sharing two faces, in a reference to the myth of the androgyne, as recounted by Aristophanes in Plato's *Symposium*. Split in half by the gods, these incomplete humans wander the earth, searching for their other halves, hoping to return to their original state of being as complete androgynous selves. This concept is expressed in the montage of animated images, accompanied by the song "The Origin of Love." The idea of people seeking wholeness through philosophical musings about original connections between nongendered human beings is a motif for the rest of the narrative.

Structured in flashbacks, this fantasy musical is interspersed with historical references to the wall separating East and West Germany and biographical details about Hedwig's own separations, including a tempestuous childhood as Hansel Schmidt (played by Ben Mayer Goodman) and a botched sex-change operation, which left her with a dysfunctional "angry inch" of flesh between her legs. Hedwig's transformation begins in East Germany, when this mere "slip of a girly boy" meets the American soldier Luther Robinson, who offers to marry Hansel, but the boy must have a sex-change operation in order to qualify for citizenship as Luther's legal wife. Hansel's mother, Hedwig, quickly agrees and transfers her name, passport, and identity to her son, who then moves to Junction City, Kansas.

The couple live happily in Kansas for a year, but on the day the Berlin Wall comes down, Luther runs off with another man. Hedwig is briefly devastated but bounces back quickly, forming a rock band with army wives born in Korea and babysitting for a fort commander. There she takes Tommy Speck under her wing and teaches him to play guitar. Teaching him everything she knows, she writes songs and dubs him "Tommy Gnosis," explaining that his last name is Greek for "knowledge." When Tommy gains knowledge of Hedwig's "angry inch," he is appalled and runs off, stealing her heart and her songs, which soon help him to become a famous rock star.

Down but not out, Hedwig brings together former eastern Europeans and her new husband, Yitzhak (Miriam Shore), to form a new "internationally ignored" band, Hedwig and the Angry Inch. The film shows them playing a series of gigs at seafood restaurants in a chain called Bilgewater's. She is suing Tommy for copyright violation, and her manager, Phyllis Stein (Andrea Martin), appears at odd moments, offering lawyerly advice about how Hedwig really should not be stalking Tommy, since she is suing him. We learn the patchwork details of Hedwig's life as she tells her story to a small coterie of younger fans and a group of bored restaurant patrons, most of whom look like annoyed retirees.

In the final scene, in a masculine persona, Hedwig stands onstage in front of Tommy, who sings to her, begging her forgiveness. At this point, she has the revelation that she has created him out of her other half. Performing at another Bilgewater's, this one on Times Square, with dazzling, white, high-key lighting, Hedwig and the band members are all glamorously dressed in white. Singing a gloriously upbeat song to "all the misfits and losers," Hedwig rips off her long blond wig and hands it to Yitzhak, who puts it on. The animated sequence at this point shows the separated halves reuniting, followed by a shot from behind of Hedwig walking nude along a dark alley, toward what appears to be a brightly lit future. This film resides on a cultural and chronological cusp, representing a melding of the campy *Rocky Horror Picture Show* musical spirit with an almost avant-garde style, including a fractured narrative, unpredictably random backstory elements, animated segments, and snapshots of real historical events. It remains as one of the classic representations that artfully captures slivers of two decades, political systems, generations, and genders.

2

BREAKING BOUNDARIES IN
THE NEW MILLENNIUM

Whereas films such as *Priscilla, Queen of the Desert, The Crying Game*, and *Boys Don't Cry* broke ground, they also received criticism for capitalizing on spectacle and exaggerating the melodrama of transgender individuals. The beginning of the new millennium witnessed a new approach, with a number of firsts in transgender cinema that gave a genuine voice and artistic agency to transgender people, exploring new settings, media, and ways of delivering content. Documentaries flourished, and successful fiction films garnered wider audiences.

Kate Davis's documentary *Southern Comfort* (2001) grabbed audiences with its directness and authenticity. Avoiding campiness, exaggeration, or voyeuristic exploitation, *Southern Comfort* encourages viewers to see the world through the eyes of Robert Eads, a transgender man in his last year of life. The film opens with a tight side-angle shot of Eads, whose lined, whiskered face and husky southern twang convey restrained emotion, immediately engaging the audience, placing us in his head, physically and emotionally. He explains how he forgives the doctors who refused to treat his ovarian cancer because he is transgender, but he worries that they are convinced they did the right thing. Perhaps they would not be so sure if they watched this documentary, which introduces us to his biological family and his chosen family of the transgender community.

The people documented in *Southern Comfort* express an interesting mix of views on sexuality, with Eads explaining that gender is not physical; it is "what's in your heart and in your mind." Although this sounds like a progressive view of sexuality, Eads also reveals occasional hints of his own biases. For example, he describes how his transgender friend's cisgender wife does not have a "lesbian bone in her body," suggesting, perhaps, some unconscious homophobia. Whether a sentiment is progressive or not, the filmmaker seems to avoid massaging or censoring any of its characters. In voice-over, Eads's father speaks of how he had always dreamed of his daughter (Eads) marrying a man who would be president, but the father is still proud to know that his daughter's heart beats inside the person who is now his son. In another scene, a transgender woman looks admiringly at herself crammed into a tight dress for the "prom" at the close of the film, saying, "I can't breathe, but I look beautiful." Without editorial comment, this statement may suggest for some viewers the societal gender standard imposed on women—whether cisgender or trans—who may feel compelled to suffer in order to be "beautiful."

New Zealand, known for a diverse culture, made history when Georgina Beyer became the first transsexual individual anywhere in the world to be elected mayor of a city (Carterton); she then became a member of Parliament. Coming from a rural and socially conservative region, Georgie had a rocky beginning in life, but this documentary reveals how she eventually wins over the hearts of her constituents and forms part of a new center-left government in 1999, serving until 2007. The film *Georgie Girl* (2002), directed by Annie Goldson and Peter Wells, tells this story with footage of Georgina talking about her life, interspersed with shots of her in the many roles she plays, including passionate and entertaining speaker, judge for sheep races, member of Parliament, and leader in Auckland's gay pride parade, waving from a float shaped like a waka, or canoe. This film about Georgina—born George Beyer—was shown on TVOne in New Zealand, SBS-TV in Australia, and Channel 4 in the United Kingdom. What distinguishes *Georgie Girl* from a number of other transgender documentaries is its lack of emphasis on the subject's transition in favor of a focus on Georgie's life and accomplishments.

Viewers learn that Georgina's background (of Pakeha, Te Ati Awa, Ngati Mutunga, Ngati Raukawa, Ngati Porou, and Anglo heritage) includes some challenging personal experiences. For a time, she was an entertainer, a sex worker, and eventually a well-known celebrity and community worker—all information presented through a blend of archival footage and first-person interviews with Georgie, friends, and neighbors. Detailing the rise of a woman described as having "grace and just something exquisite about her," *Georgie Girl* is structured in a way that reveals her final success early on in the film, when a friend declares that in "a few more years, she could be the prime minister," which is exactly what happens.

A mélange of footage and photos from George Beyer's past reveals a person who always had an androgynous quality, as Georgina describes herself: "I always looked quite feminine. I was a late developer, never developed facial hair." Georgina comments, "I got terribly confident, went prancing off into town. Out in public being a woman. That made me feel far more comfortable." Drawn to acting, Georgie often acted in school, taking the last name of Beyer from her mother's successful second husband, a law-school graduate. Georgie left school at fifteen to pursue an acting career, against her mother's wishes, and for a time she lived on welfare, which was difficult as long as she presented herself as a woman. Officials would tell her, " 'Put your trousers back on and get back out there and work.' I stood my ground; I wasn't going to change that for anybody." This almost random flashback technique is fascinating, but it does make it somewhat difficult to sort out a clear timeline for Georgie's stages in transition. This looseness may well be deliberate, in order to convey the sense of rootless searching during this part of Georgie's life.

After discovering The Balcony drag-show cabaret, Georgie begins to blossom, displaying her singing and acting talent: "It was as if I had arrived home and seen the light." The club was popular with gay and straight people, and part of the appeal was guessing which entertainers were men or women. Here, the film includes inserted snippets of archival footage from the drag scene and cultural milieu, interspersed with women talking about how female hormones make them "think and act like women." Georgie talks about transitioning to a female state when she begins hormone treatment, thinking at the time that the more she "took, the quicker it would happen, which wasn't so." Throughout this sequence, others describe how she is "strikingly beautiful" and endowed with "confidence, guts, pizzazz."

Georgie looks back on a time when she was a sex worker and was sexually assaulted by two men, describing how she began to think about what she could do to help others who had no representation, because she "would be the only person with firsthand knowledge of the sex industry." As Georgie begins to transition, she visits her mother, who is dying of cancer. The caregiver asks Georgie's mother if Georgie is her daughter, but the mother insists that Georgie is her son. This event seems to signal a new life for Georgie, and the film shifts to bucolic shots of country scenes, with the voice-over of Georgie's hauntingly beautiful voice singing "Summertime." As she walks along with other transsexuals, the scene gives the sense that she is blossoming into the sweetest period of her life. With Georgie's sex-change operation in 1984, she finds that the life of a transsexual is not without peril. She describes how she was once given a ride by a truck driver who held a knife to her throat. Her friend describes how "like any true queen she got her revenge. With another queen, they beat the shit out of him," left him with no clothes, and told him to "bugger off." After living in Australia, Georgie decides to go back to New Zealand and work on her acting career, receiving a GOFTA Award nomination in 1987 for her part in *Jewel's Darl*. She observes that she was not overwhelmed with offers, and she finds herself typecast as a transsexual rather than being able to perform a variety of roles. Her dissatisfaction with this situation presents an interesting conundrum, given the current demand among many performers who argue that transgender actors, rather than cisgendered ones, should be selected for transgender roles.

The film takes a sunnier tone when it focuses on Georgina's blossoming role as a community leader when she moves to the small town of Carterton, Wairarapa, where she watches children cling to the backs of huge sheep in a sheep-riding contest and strolls through the small streets and paths of her new home. This move to a rural community offers her an opportunity to work as a news announcer and radio host for Paul Henry's FM 89.3 station. As Georgie becomes involved in mainstream education, she engages with her community and helps troubled young people, who perform with talent and enthusiasm in a theater performance directed by Georgie. She explains how her past experience as a troubled teen and later as a sex worker gives her sympathy for outcasts in society. Gradually, Georgie impresses most of the people in Carterton, and she becomes a council member and eventually mayor. A few years later, after repeated invitations to run for the national office of member of Parliament, she takes on the challenge.

Campaigning in a vast territory with a relatively small population, Georgie gets to know voters, and for most people, to know her is to love her. On election night, footage reveals her as a nervous candidate awaiting the results. In voice-over, she explains how she did not want to talk to anyone or be comforted over the initial returns, which seemed to forecast a humiliating loss. Later in the evening, when she finally gets word that she has won, she is ecstatic. In her triumphant first appearance in Parliament, she appears, beautifully dressed and coiffed, and introduces herself with a humorous quip that wins over her peers. After this triumphant moment, however, the film ends on a somewhat reflective note. She muses on how dedication to her career has caused her to give up any dreams of having a romantic partner, for fear of the ways he might be judged. This element of down-to-earth realism reminds the viewer that the life of the transsexual— even one as talented and determined as Georgie—still has challenges that cisgendered people are seldom forced to consider. This touching authenticity makes the film more complex than the typical happy-ending biopic, but it also offers hope and inspiration.

Whereas a number of early films have the transition process as a focus, films of the new millennium have shifted to other aspects of transgender experience in specifically focused topic films. In 2004, the transgender filmmaker Tara Mateik worked with the Sylvia Rivera Law Project to release the video *Toilet Training*, which documents the ways transgender people are verbally and physically harassed and sometimes assaulted by transphobic people. The film suggests public policies that would create a more inclusive environment for transgender people in schools, work environments, and public buildings. A number of libraries and institutions have adopted this film to enhance diversity training, fight discrimination, and improve the culture of our schools and public spaces for gender-nonconforming individuals.

In a film that captures elements of Filipino culture that may be new to Western viewers, Auraeus Solito's *The Blossoming of Maximo Oliveros* (2005) opens in what seems to be a realist style. Opening with shots of an unspecified city that could be any town in the Philippines and using cinema verité techniques, the filmmaker creates a sense of immersion in a vibrant culture, alive with motion, sound, and constant movement. The first shot of garbage floating in a pond is accompanied by a male voice singing "This Is My Country," in English: "I cannot stay away from here, I cannot leave her alone, because I love her." A close-up of a delicate, braceleted hand picking up a magenta orchid from garbage strewn on the ground tilts up to a passing train and then back down to a flower-draped hearse passing by in the street below. Through a montage sequence that Sergei Eisenstein would admire, Solito presents the viewer with a dialectical set of images that convey beauty, poverty, innocence, and modernity in rapid succession. Another shot focuses on a pair of youthful legs and feet with an ankle bracelet, pausing as children pass by. Finally, we catch a glimpse from the side of what appears to be a young girl, leaning over a tangle of beads in a shop.

The setting is the Philippines, and the young protagonist, Maxi, is shopping in the outdoor stands of the marketplace. In a slow tilt up, the camera frames a flouncy, pink chiffon dress and then cuts to a close-up of Maximo, an androgynous adolescent of about thirteen, wearing a headband and a flower perched over one ear, smiling with a three-quarter flirtatious tilt of his head and looking straight into the camera—the only time the filmmaker breaks the fourth wall. After a brief clip of someone playing a rickety piano, the camera follows Maximo from behind, through herds of children, as the youth passes with an exaggerated swaying walk, wearing a pink-flowered short skirt and a blue cap-sleeved shirt. Maximo sashays past a group of men, and one of them teases, "Who you been flirting with?" to which the youth mugs, waggles his head defiantly, and shakes his hand dismissively over his shoulder as he turns and walks on. By this point, it is clear that Maximo is a young boy, but the gender cues of clothing, voice, and gesture indicate a different internal identification for his character.

Cutting back briefly to the man playing the broken piano, a bird's-eye shot reveals him slumping in frustration over the keyboard. The next scene establishes the central family as a single-gender group with Maxi as the only feminine presence. Here, Maxi's father and two brothers sit at a table waiting for Maxi to serve them. When Maxi serves the father, he taunts his two sons, saying that Maxi serves him, not them, and then hands Maxi some cash, casually suggesting that he go and buy some sanitary pads. The other brother asks jokingly for pads with wings. This exchange is done in good humor as if it is the common mode of communication for the family. Night falls, and the scene shifts to a living-room gathering where the men watch a video while Maxi tries to untangle a string of lights. Maxi asks how they can watch such a noisy program, and one brother answers that it is a way to avoid thinking. They all demonstrate their limited literacy as they try to sound out the title: *Schemer*. This name is ironic, given that this family schemes for a living, figuring out illegal ways to fence stolen goods and run other kinds of scams, while Maxi cares for them as a codependent abused spouse might do. While Maxi looks longingly out the light-festooned window, his father tenderly picks up a small picture of his wife and dusts it, both generations longing for an unreachable dream.

The next vignettes reveal the relative freedom of Maxi's social world, in which childhood and adult activities intermingle. Morning begins with upbeat guitar music and shots of Maxi cleaning up cigarette butts from the night before, but when he sees a man entering the room downstairs, he races down to capture a glimpse of him preparing for sex with a very willing young woman or, more probably, a prostitute. When the door is slammed in his face, he goes out into the street and—as if in retaliation for his recent rejection—grabs a little boy, forcibly bathing him until his mother comes to pick him up.

A self-reflexive interior scene captures the chaos of Maxi's life, through a mishmash of cheap melodramatic images in videos that Maxi and a group of children are watching. A properly dressed school boy arrives and questions what he is doing, and Maxi leaves to buy bottles of water with the money from his father. He calls to his fellow "girls" to follow him to get costumes for a Miss Universe pageant, all accompanied by the disco tune of "Mr. Wao." The Bollywood-style act is interrupted by an almost surreal performance of a boy finding his mother dead on the floor and saying that she is as cold as the noodles. In a mock interview segment of the children's beauty contest, the emcee asks Maxi, "What is love?" a question that jolts him into remembering that he has to serve food to his family. It is no accident that this particular question spurs him to remember his role in "real" life—to play mother to the all-male family that he loves.

The narrative switches to a more somber subject matter and color palette, as several young men entrap Maxi and start to strip him, apparently in preparation for rape. Screaming, Maxi is rescued by a policeman named Victor, who shames and chases away the would-be attackers. Maxi's character suddenly appears childlike, draped over the large shoulders of the handsome policeman, who carries him home piggyback, whistling the "Mr. Wao" song. When they enter the apartment, the brothers suggest that the incident was Maxi's fault for flirting with his attackers, and Victor says he will notify the boys' families of their behavior. The father thrusts money at him, but Victor replies that he is just doing his job, while a shot of Maxi shows the look of love on his face. Following Victor out, Maxi affectionately calls him "Kuya," or big brother, and the policeman tells him, "Don't stay out late, okay?" When Maxi's real brother returns, covered in blood, the implication is clear.

At this point, the narrative is in a tangle, visually signaled by a shot of clustered electrical wires against the cloudy morning sky, at the start of a troubled climactic day. The father insists that Maxi can only go out with his family, and as one brother flirts with a young woman and says he is not free, she passes Maxi with a look of disgust on her face. The brother walks on, his arm draped protectively over his brother's shoulder until Maxi pairs up with an effeminate friend. Back home, all the boys fall asleep watching a romantic movie, *Anak* (2000), and the older man wipes his eyes. In another vignette, when a group of children laugh as they look down on a couple of nude boys in a pile of leaves, the film makes light of their sexual play. The narrative takes a more serious turn when Maxi sees his brother trying to wash blood out of a shirt. At this point, Victor comes by their place, and then Maxi silently follows Victor into a church, where Victor kneels to pray as Maxi looks on, the two faces in profile in the dark interior. This moment shows the young officer's influence on the boy, suggesting that Victor is his first positive role model.

In the growing intimacy of the relationship between Maxi and Victor, Maxi presents himself as an ideal wife substitute, while Victor maintains the role of big brother. When Victor buys Maxi some food, the young boy says he is such a good cook that the policeman will forget his "girlfriend's name." The father and brother look on from behind, suspicious of the man's intentions, while Maxi unintentionally reveals that his father sells stolen cell phones for a living. The policeman tells Maxi to get a job that he can be proud of when he grows up, and when the boy replies that he wants to sell DVDs, Victor says to be sure they are not pirated. Maxi asks if Victor could not make an exception for him, but he answers that "wrong is wrong." Later on, a mirror shot shows Maxi putting on red lipstick and a red headband before serving his family dinner. When the police stop by to ask them about a murder, they all claim no knowledge, but a slow zoom on Maxi's sad face reveals that he knows that his brother is the killer. A shot of Maxi burning the shirt confirms the viewer's suspicion.

Still a child, Maxi appears to forget the family troubles as the camera captures him in the morning light, flouncing along as usual in a girlish outfit. Running into another boy-girl who says s/he has to go to church, Maxi looks scornful and goes on his way, exaggerating the sway of his hips even more. When he sees Victor, he follows him home and insists on cleaning his filthy house for him, playing housewife to the young man. Victor asks Maxi how his father and brother treat him, and Maxi replies cheerfully that he only gets an occasional smack and some teasing, "but they're cool." Maxi sits on the bed beside Victor, who is wearing a white shirt with a cross dangling conspicuously on his chest. When he shows Maxi a picture of his deceased father, Maxi asks why he looks like a priest, and Victor replies that it is only because his father is wearing white. An undertone of slight emotional or sexual tension occurs when Maxi touches a scar on Victor's face and asks how he got it, but the older man ignores the question and quickly changes the mood by suggesting that they go outside. Once they leave Victor's room, sexual tension is displaced onto a humorous lesson on how to whistle, but, like the famous scene of Lauren Bacall telling Humphrey Bogart in *To Have and Have Not* (1944) to "just put your lips together and blow," whistling lessons are never without a subtext.

The importance of education is another more obvious subtext of the film, and as Maxi watches his classmates going to school, Victor asks if the boy does not miss it. Maxi explains defiantly that his father says no one can take advantage of their family, going on to boast that when he was at school, he used to make Peter jealous for being the teachers' favorite. To spur him to go back to school, Victor says that Peter must be their favorite now. The young actor's sideways glance reflects beautifully the second thoughts his character is having.

Conversations between Victor and Maxi deepen at this point in the narrative. As part of Maxi's attempt to woo Victor, Maxi asks him if he has a girlfriend. The reply is, "Do you see me with anyone?" to which Maxi answers with a triumphant grin, "Only me." Victor asks what he knows about these things, and Maxi replies that he is already twelve, and his "friends already have boyfriends." Victor comments on "how times have changed" but then persists in his efforts to heterosexualize Maxi's behavior by asking Maxi when he will get a girlfriend. The boy replies, "Yuchh . . . gross," and in a surprising backtrack, Victor simply says, without apparent judgment, "It's a boyfriend you want." This exchange ends with Maxi returning home, looking at himself in the mirror and wiping off his lipstick, an action that seems to signal a turning point in their relationship.

The sinister side of the family's criminal activities pulls Maxi further into a sense of responsibility and hopelessness. Paco is arrested for selling drugs. Attempting to knit Victor into the family, the brothers ask the policeman to drink with them, but he declines and leaves. The family discusses having Victor killed, while Maxi stands silent and thoughtful. The next day, he goes to take lunch to Victor at the police station, where Victor tells Maxi he saw someone burning a shirt. The next scene shows the father beating his son and yelling, "I raised you a thief but not a murderer!" After the father and brothers beat Victor and threaten to kill him, Maxi sneaks into his apartment to care for him. A series of dissolves show Maxi sniffling as he wipes away the blood and takes off Victor's shirt. The scene closes with a fade-out on Maxi, who cradles Victor's bloody head as he sleeps.

In a daring voyeuristic scene, the camera shows Maxi awakening in sunlight and looking into the shower to see

Victor nude. Maxi watches with palpable longing as Victor slowly and painfully dons underwear over his smooth, muscled legs. As they sit together, Victor softly strokes the boy's head, but when Maxi plants a quick kiss on Victor's cheek, Victor tells him to go home; his family must be looking for him. The film conveys Maxi's sense of being head over heels in love by showing him performing cartwheels, accompanied by an upbeat musical soundtrack, with a 180-degree circling of the camera as it points up to blue skies and fluffy, white clouds. This dream is quickly undercut when he arrives home and his father berates him: "Take care of other people but not your own family." His brothers complain that he forgot the salt and then comment on his glum mood: "Must be his monthly period." The family confronts Victor in the street, but Maxi secretly goes to leave a note on his door, only to find it ignored later on.

Eventually Victor tells Maxi to find someone his own age: "I don't have time for this." With the arrival of a new chief of police, Victor takes on the brutality and bullying of his fellow police, and Maxi's brother offers advice: "Forget him, show him that you're strong. He's not the only guy in the world." When the police raid the family's home and find stolen private CDs, Maxi clings to his mother's dress. After Victor puts Maxi's brother in jail, the father complains, "Why do we have to live like this?

You never complained before. Victor comes along, and you're ashamed of us. Your mother would be angry. Is he more important than us? I want life to be peaceful. Isn't there another way? I work like a dog. I'm not going to lose another member of this family." When Maxi sees that the family gun is gone, he leaves to make sure Victor will not be killed, but then he witnesses his father shot by the police, his body spread in a Christ-like pose on the street.

Back at the police station, Victor is shown doing paperwork and looking at himself in a mirror in a moment of apparent self-reflection. The police eventually free Maxi's brother without charges, and meanwhile at home, Maxi cries and makes rice. Victor tells Maxi, "The world is full of evil men. Sometimes you have to play their game, or nothing will change. Do you understand?" Maxi replies, "Yes. There are many evil men, but I only had one father." Maxi leaves wordlessly as children play in background, returning home, where an interior shot shows Maxi kneeling with a box of his father's belongings. When he hears whistling outside, he looks out the window, and the camera reveals that it is Victor below in the street. Maxi whistles back, and the fact that he can now whistle reflects his maturation and the passage of time. As they whistle to each other, a profile shot of Victor reveals tears streaming down his cheek. In a suggestion that Maxi is now the one in a position of power, the boy looks out the window but does not go down. Victor leaves, and the camera lingers on a shot of the empty window. With the passage of time, the household changes, and in the next sequence, the brothers are ironing for themselves and cooking. They instruct Maxi to pin his name tag on his school uniform, as pictures of mother and father sit on the shelf in the background. Handing him his lunch and backpack, one says, "My sister is so pretty. Pay attention in class." These words follow the pattern of teasing Maxi for his effeminacy, but they have an element of tenderness, pride, and concern for his success. The closing scene shows Maxi looking sharp in his freshly ironed uniform, on his way to school. Victor's car passes by Maxi, who does not look at him. Up ahead, the car stops, and Victor gets out, standing by the car smoking as the boy approaches. Maxi passes by, resolutely ignoring Victor. For just a moment, he slows, and then he picks up the pace again, walking on. This ambiguous ending signals the boy's independence and maturation, but it is not clear exactly what final shape Maxi's "blossoming" will eventually take.

During the first decade of the 2000s, progress continued in a variety of ways with participation of trans artists and cisgender allies. Gwen Haworth's *She's a Boy I Knew* (2006) marks the first film for which a transgender subject also serves as camera operator. In *A Girl like Me: The Gwen Araujo Story* (2006), the cisgender Polish director

Agnieszka Holland worked with the writer Shelley Evans and the actors Mercedes Ruehl, J. D. Pardo, and Lupe Ontiveros to tell the true story of the 2002 murder of a young transgender woman. The film won the GLAAD award for outstanding film for television in 2006. In 2008, Kortney Ryan Ziegler wrote and directed *Still Black: A Portrait of Black Transmen*, to contribute another transgender perspective to the growing body of trans cinema. Also in 2008, Eliza Greenwood, the lesbian sister of a deaf trans man released a film conveying her brother's life experience, *Austin Unbound* (2011), bringing the often neglected and stereotyped disabled community into the mix.

Boy I Am, directed by Sam Feder and Julie Hollar, offers an excellent primer for anyone interested in exploring the intersection between FTM transgender people and various feminist and lesbian communities. This exploration takes viewers down a winding path, while juggling a number of balls simultaneously: stories of four FTM individuals; reactions of their partners; a history of intellectual and ideological conflicts among FTM, feminist, and lesbian communities; and the roles of organizations, social movements, and medical support structures. Perhaps in an attempt to create a dialectic or a set of snapshot impressions, the filmmakers jump from one speaker to the next, with only briefly displayed captions identifying individuals. The speakers themselves discuss views that change over time, so it is sometimes challenging to pin down where their sympathies or opinions reside at any given moment.

Early on, however, the filmmakers lay down several foundational statements of profound significance to discussions about bodies, texts, and gender: "Everybody has a modified body," "we read each other's bodies all the time," and there is "not a person on the planet who has an exclusively female identity or male identity." As one of the most prominent transgender scholars in the film, Judith Jack Halberstam offers background analysis of the opposition between trans communities and feminism, as discussed in Janice Raymond's controversial book *The Transsexual Empire*. In this volume, Raymond argues that surgical and psychological "solutions" to "transsexualism" bolster gender stereotypes and turn gender identity into a medical or psychiatric "condition." Sensitive to the bias in favor of masculinity inherent in most cultures, Raymond critiques patriarchal "making of woman according to man's image" as a means of colonizing "feminist identification, culture, politics and sexuality" (101–2). The highly inflammatory statements in this book do not reflect Raymond's later views, and in a 2014 interview (Vigo), she recants one of her most divisive metaphors: "All transsexuals rape women's bodies by reducing the real female form to an artifact, appropriating this body for themselves," when they "merely cut off the most obvious means of invading women, so that they seem noninvasive" (Raymond 101–2). Halberstam lays a good deal of responsibility for a split between the lesbian and trans communities on Raymond's work, and some statements made throughout *Boy I Am* suggest that these tensions persist to varying degrees among different groups. For example, Bernadette McHenry discuss how some "butch fems" viewed transitioning as a form of selling out by abandoning the unpopular masculine female body.

Feder and Hollar's film takes a nuanced approach, and it includes thoughtful concerns about FTM use of hormonal and surgical transitions, counterbalanced by those who affirm the supremacy of transgender rights, and the importance of controlling one's own body, regardless of age. It also discusses frankly the practice of breast binding, which one subject, Nicco, describes as feeling "liberating at first" but later as causing "tissue damage and bruised ribs." He speaks of how "physical pain becomes so fused with . . . mental pain" that one wonders, "What have I gotten myself into?" The film also considers the classism inherent in some transgender individuals having the luxury to have a surgery that costs about $7,450, while others must remain in a body that does not fit their own sense of identity. Keegan, who considers the challenge of costs, comes from a large, Catholic, working-class family, and his only way to get the money is through a Kickstarter campaign. Carmen Vasquez, a male-identified lesbian, explains how surgery was never an appealing option for her: "The body thing has never been an issue with me. I think of myself as a male-identified woman. It's an issue for butch-identified women," who may feel confused or conflicted.

In the film, Halberstam discusses the question of an appropriate age for FTM surgery, explaining that at one time, trans people were described as primary or secondary, to distinguish people who identified as the opposite gender in early childhood from those who expressed this identification later on as a teen or adult. In making the body more masculine, an individual has more opportunity and is "more culturally valued." Elizabeth Cline discusses how one of the fundamental battles of feminism has been "coming to terms with our bodies," but for trans people, "it's about not coming to terms with your body, choosing to become another type of body." While women are "struggling with all these issues, . . . someone has the audacity to drop $20,000 to have breasts removed." Keegan disagrees onscreen with feminists who claim that FTM transgender males are undermining their progress: "I don't think of myself as undoing what butch-identified women have done." Saying that some women may not understand how he can identify with a male body, he declares that in spite of his female biological origins, "Boy I am."

The film blends statements about these philosophical issues with the experience of anticipating surgery. Nicco claims that transitioning through surgery is the "art of becoming who we are," and his discussion of the upcoming surgery reveals his anticipation. On the eve of top surgery, he describes feeling "so excited about going clothes shopping" and about it being "the last day" he has "to wear a sports bra." He says, "I own my body now. I don't have to obsess over it all the time." Norrie expresses more ambivalence, and his girlfriend, Lucey, talks about the implications of his transition, describing how she had to overcome some issues with men in order to adapt to Norrie's more masculine body. When asked if she would have liked Norrie as a man, she says she thinks she would have. She values the "intimate opportunity of being with a trans man" and "letting go of that [feminine] part of him." Softening her assessment, Norrie says that he is "not a man yet" but feels more like a teenager whose voice still cracks: "I'll still keep a lot of my feminine characteristics." He declares that it seems like something he wishes he "would have done sooner."

The film also looks at more long-term consequences of transition. Fifteen months after top surgery, Keegan describes himself as "a trans person, heterosexual dude," but says that this identity "turns people off" because of a "strange policing within the trans community. You have to be this kind of boy." With regard to family acceptance, the differences between Keegan's experience and Norrie's are striking. Keegan describes how his large, traditional Catholic family was totally accepting: "The reason I decided to go with it after all the back and forth . . . was because of no apparent reason. It felt really good. My family has been pretty awesome," even though they are "hard-core hard-knocks, all like sixty, seventy": "I couldn't imagine how this was going to be." He reports that they all had the same response: "You're family." One aunt told him that his girlfriend was gorgeous: "They'd never seen me so happy." In contrast, Norrie, an African American, says, "family is the ultimate obstacle for me." His family refuses to see him as a man. He comments, "Not one person has acknowledged that I'm a man. I don't care. I've never had a close relationship." He comes to the conclusion, "When things aren't going right, you have to fix them for yourself." Norrie says that his family was not able to see how hard it was for him to be a girl.

The relationship of masculinity to the lesbian community is explored in some courageous and controversial ways in the film, particularly on the issue of an appropriate age for transition. Vasqez expresses concerns that "young bodies that are still growing don't know what they are or what they want": "If there's pressure from a peer group, I worry sometimes that maybe they're getting pressure at too young an age." Halberstam recommends that people "take the time to live in this body, know this body," and recounts her own experience: "I was very uncomfortable with my body at nineteen; I hadn't had a lot of good sex. If someone offers T (testosterone) at nineteen, I'm on it; it would have seemed like the answer to my problems." Explaining that "we come to understand our sexuality through some of our sexual practices," in a culture in which "girls aren't comfortable with their bodies," Halberstam concludes, "I think this stuff is really premature."

Although the trans people profiled in *Boy I Am* all think of themselves as male and want to be male, they express ambivalence because of the characteristics associated with masculinity in Western patriarchal societies. Norrie says, "One fear I have is being a black male. Having to deal with the stereotypes, the general fear. . . . I don't really want to be a huge macho man." Not all of the subjects present the same viewpoints, and with the FTM versus feminism debate, or conflicting relationships between trans and butch, rigid identity politics emerge as the culprit. The film closes on a note of reconciliation, after presenting a number of conflicting views, noting that feminism has fought for decades against the idea that biology is destiny. The film offers a recommendation to "think about how to build alliances to those communities" in an effort to connect reproductive care, women's struggles, and an end to the "painful exclusion trans men experience with lesbian communities." Emphasizing the need for a "movement for social and political justice," *Boy I Am* closes on an optimistic note: "Our well-being is connected to the well-being of all people who are oppressed. This is the last frontier." At the same time, there is a visual of a placard that reads, "Transjustice Now."

In a more straightforward narrative, the Canadian documentary *Girl Inside* (2007) follows Matthew on a three-year journey to becoming Madison. In this film, Maya Gallus documents Madison's quest for biological womanhood, beginning with estrogen treatments. She describes herself as always having felt like she was "part of a different crowd," with friends who were disabled, gay, and a variety of other socially marginalized categories. At first, Madison speaks into the camera, confessing, "I wouldn't let myself admit that I wanted to be a girl." As she begins her journey toward transition, she turns to her grandmother, a youthful eighty-year-old who is quite accepting of Madison's decision. She tries to instruct Madison and help her enhance the feminine aspects of her appearance, but a generation gap is evident when she tries to put Madison's hair in rollers or get her to wear jewelry. Acknowledging that a number of social clues and key indicators cause people to perceive masculine or feminine gender, Madison decides that the first surgical step will be to have surgery to reduce the size of her Adam's apple, at a cost of $3,000.

This is one of the most informative films about the nitty-gritty details of transitioning to a female physique, and many of the more pointed questions come from Madison's grandmother. She wonders aloud how a surgeon can possibly re-create female genitalia, given the complexity of this equipment. The grandmother supports Madison during the first transitional year, taking her to swim in an ocean, even though she dreads the thought of her penis showing through her soaked swim trunks. Although the grandmother accepts fairly readily, when Madison goes to visit her mother after a year of hormone therapy, their first exchange is more fraught with emotion and sadness. As Madison arrives at her mother's place, slow motion mimics the hesitation that Madison no doubt feels at this moment, perhaps wishing time would slow down or feeling the passage of time as expanding out into an eternity as she worries about this encounter. Madison's mother is fairly direct as she explains that after knowing Madison as her son for twenty-five years, "it takes some time to give up that person," to figure out "how to get from here to there": "I gave birth to a son. I raised that son. My son

Matthew is not really there anymore." Madison is less sentimentally attached to her former self. For example, she describes her Adam's apple as "a throwback to who [she] used to be, so it's time to get rid of it."

Madison's grandmother explains that when Madison first acknowledged her feelings, she assumed that since "she thought she was a woman, everyone else should feel this way." During the period when Madison is saving up for surgery, she decides to go online and try to date, presenting herself as a woman. She struggles with deciding when to let a man know she is transsexual, explaining that she does not want to put this information in her profile because she does not want "chasers," or people who "fetishize transsexuals." Madison has a complex understanding of her feelings toward issues of gender. She develops a semiromantic relationship with a boy who had been her friend when she was Matthew, but she does not want to consummate any sexual relationship as long as she has a penis. She comments that this may reflect "internalized homophobia, fear of being gay," for she sees herself "completely as a woman, especially in bed." After a moment of reflection, she adds, "Entering my penis into the equation, it would mess with my sense of gender too badly."

Madison's greatest difficulty is talking to her mother, father, sister, and brother about her decision. After speaking to them on the phone, she visits, and the camera captures their responses in a way that makes them seem spontaneous and unrehearsed. Although parts of the film look like reenactments designed to further the story, the interviews with parents and siblings have a spontaneous look and feel. In voice-over, we hear the father describing how emotions are "not something you can switch a switch on." He found himself wondering, "What did I do wrong? I did a lot of research. At work there are a couple of guys that are gay. A friend of theirs has had this. I learned a lot." As the father sits talking with Madison, he tries to make light of the situation by humorous descriptions of the situation, singsonging, "Madison wants a vagina." Piggybacking on her father's metaphor, Madison says with an almost bitter undertone, "All I want for Christmas is my two front testicles—gone!" To which the dad replies, "I'm glad she's got the balls to do what she's doin' while she's still got 'em." His brave and good-willed attempt to be completely accepting is undercut by his nervousness and his clear misunderstanding of how to say the right thing.

The scene changes to an outdoor setting without Madison's presence. In direct address to the interviewer, gazing into the camera in a tight close-up shot, the father says, "We all change, day by day, some more than others," laughing nervously. He goes on to say what he thinks he should say, what may be true, for the most part: "I'm real happy for Madison because Madison's happy. What more can a father want than to have your kid happy? That's it." Taking a deep breath, he turns his face down and to the side, trying to compose himself, a look of grief replacing the smile for a moment before he turns back to the camera and grins, tears in his eyes. This scene is the emotional pay dirt of the film, when viewers get a glimpse into the family in the background witnessing Madison's struggle.

An insert shot of a wind chime in the rain and fall leaves floating in water underscores the feeling of loss that both parents express, before we turn to the next great emotional hurdle. In voice-over, Madison talks about her anxiety over seeing her sister and brother, even though she has informed them about her gender identity. She has even sent a picture of herself to her sister, the second person she tells after her grandmother. Her sister immediately accepts Madison's decision, saying that she would not have been surprised if she learned that Madison was gay. The film adds a moment of suspense by including a misunderstanding that offers some comic relief. On the phone, Madison's sister, who is preparing for her wedding, asks, "Does this mean you're going to be a bridesmaid instead of a groomsman? Damn!" Madison recounts how at this point she did not know how to interpret the reaction: "I said, 'Ach, what does that mean?' and then my sister explained, 'Well we had the right number of groomsmen and bridesmaids. Now we're off,' and I thought, 'Oh my god, Maggie, I so love you.'" As the camera captures the sister showing Madison her wedding dress, the sister says in voice-over, "I trust her and the fact that I know that if she says she's female and she knows she's a woman, then that's enough for me." Admiring the dress, Madison holds up her finger and thumb, saying, "I'm just a little bit jealous. Just a little bit."

In preparation for the next reunion scene, Madison confesses to being much more nervous about meeting her brother, Ryan, for the first time since she came out with her feminine identity. They hug, somewhat awkwardly, and Ryan says he is "extremely nervous." As Ryan prepares to go out for his birthday celebration, it becomes clear that Madison is not invited to join in. In a profile shot of Madison driving away, she says, "I won't hold it against him." Rationalizing that if everyone finds out she "is a tranny, it will probably be a thing," she explains his behavior: "He works in a factory, so a lot of the guys are 'men's' men. I know they make a lot of gay jokes; it's that kind of an atmosphere. It still makes me feel like shit. If I was my old self, I'd be invited, no questions asked. I'm not quite normal." After this bittersweet meeting with family, the final portion of the film skims over the long year of waiting and working to save enough money for the surgery, which comes in just under $17,000 in Canada. In order to approve surgery, Madison must have two letters, from a surgeon and a psychiatrist. An impatient Madison describes how she feels no hesitation about her choice—only impatience and a desire to complete the process: "I just keep thinking it's because of that little bit of flesh. If it hadn't been there, I would have had a normal life."

Insert shots of pink blossoms suggest the passage of time, perhaps a hint of femininity and the rebirth of spring, when Madison begins dating a young man who was a longtime friend. She talks about how "he was there to help" her, and the boy explains, "I think of her as female. This has actually confused me. I was able to go over to thinking of her as completely female. I don't try to imagine they're not there. I don't see gender as just physical anymore." Madison skirts the issue of just how far they have gone physically, simply saying, "He just completely sees me as a woman. We've had long conversations." This period is clearly a struggle, in which they have disagreements and worries about money. Stress seems to be a factor in Madison's experiencing chest pains and difficulty breathing, which turn out not to be actual heart problems. Meanwhile, Madison second-guesses her choice, saying, "I do think I've got this thing down here that just looks wrong. If there was no surgery, I could try self-love. I have the urge to just rip the damn thing off."

The film frankly addresses possible drawbacks of surgery, and the grandmother wants to know how satisfied Madison will be with the results, even if the surgeon is a genius: "That is the thing I find intriguing and puzzling. How on earth can someone sculpt something like that?" She tells Madison that this is the most crucial thing she will ever do, like getting married. Madison maintains that having the surgery out of the way "is going to be a great relief." Commenting on her disbelief that this is actually going to happen, Madison describes her upcoming surgery as "like skydiving." When asked how this procedure can take only two hours, the handsome, young, French Canadian surgeon explains that if he were inexperienced, it might take four to six hours, but since he has "done a thousand of those surgeries," he could go through the process like someone singing a well-rehearsed song. The scene closes with a shot of a mermaid doll, making the subtle point that something will be missing from Madison's physique, but she may still feel like a fish out of water for a while, at least. As Madison goes under, a burnout transition to white indicates her loss of consciousness. A strong heartbeat sounds as a blank whiteness fills the screen, which then cuts to a shot of Madison getting ready to skydive. The camera follows her fall as she leaps from the plane. A long beep sounds ominously like a signal of flatlining, but then we see Madison lying on the bed in post-op, surrounded by her mother, grandmother, and boyfriend: "She's a girl now. Maddy. This morning. Today." This sound and visual montage presents the event as a kind death and rebirth.

Recovery is depicted as presenting the usual post-operative challenges associated with any major surgery—faintness when she tries to walk, difficulty urinating, and some bleeding at suture points. Fairly quickly, the narrative flashes forward to Madison bragging to her grandmother about riding a bicycle again, and we see her romping along almost like a child, as if nothing has happened. In describing how she is preparing for a new life, she acknowledges that the way may not be smooth: "I don't want to be seen as a transsexual. I want to be seen as just a woman." As she and her boyfriend embrace, some viewers (and probably her grandmother as well) may be left wondering about the physical intimacy of their relationship, but the film offers no details. Rather, it shifts to more anodyne plans for a life together: "Cameron and I would love to have a bit of land, chickens for some eggs." Madison closes by philosophizing about the possibilities for reincarnation, asserting that her "life is to learn what it is to be trans." If she does not learn to accept and understand who she is, she envisions herself simply being born transsexual again, until she finally gets it right and moves on to an unknown future life or perhaps a bodiless realm of enlightened nothingness.

Céline Sciamma's fiction film *Tomboy* (2011) gives away the French film's premise by its title, but Zoé Héran is perfectly androgynous playing first a preteen named Laure and then a self-invented boy named Mickäel. As in *The Blossoming of Maximo Oliveros*, the film opens not with a traditional establishing shot but with a fragmented view of the subject, revealing body parts and physical background rather than a clear setting or entire body of the protagonist. Viewers meet the child in disorienting opening shots that present the back of her head, a disembodied hand waving in the breeze. The symbolic import of this fragmented view of the character emerges upon reflection and in retrospect, as one looks back over the narrative. We realize that this child is standing up looking out from the sunroof of a car, engrossed in the moment but trusting an adult to guide this powerful machine. In the next shots, the camera maintains the point of view of Laure, who sits on the lap of her father (Mathieu Demy), steering the car. The metaphor of a child allowed to steer the car foreshadows this child's attempts to maneuver her way through the complicated waters of gender identification on her own. The mother ends up offering some harsh guidance along the way, producing a rather bumpy landing for Laure's flight of fancy.

When the family moves to a new town and a girl named Lisa (Jeanne Disson) asks Laure's name, Laure decides to style herself as Mickäel. Later on, an impromptu game of steal the flag provides an entrée into the child community, and Mikael establishes himself as a winner, with a little help from Lisa, who covertly whispers to him to take it, allowing him to steal the flag and gain victory for his team. That evening, playing in the bathtub, doing a fake interview with a showerhead, Mickäel shampoos the long, dark locks of his little sister, Jeanne (Malonn Lévana). After Mickäel's declaration of masculinity, this scene takes on an added edge that a shot of two sisters in a tub would probably not have. It is also interesting that when Mikael speaks to his mother (Sophie Cattani), his voice seems a little deeper and less modulated than hers, signaling a masculine tinge to his persona. It is difficult to say whether this lower timbre is simply natural to the child actor or the director has coached the young performer to deepen her voice. Lisa is alone among the children in having obvious signs of puberty, with small but noticeable breasts. They are an intimate and easygoing mixed-race group, occasionally discussing sexual matters using childish vocabulary. Lisa is the natural leader, larger and appearing to be older and more commanding than the other children, most of whom are boys, especially in scenes of sports or games. Two other small girls are occasionally pictured isolated, amusing themselves quietly apart from the others. Playing a version of truth or dare, Mickäel is forced to take Lisa's gum and chew it, with a look of covert pleasure.

The film keeps casting the protagonist in a situation that emphasizes the gap between male freedoms and female restrictions, even among children. At one point, Mickäel watches wistfully as some of the boys remove their shirts, prompting his desire to appear more masculine. Lisa asks why he does not want to play, and later at home, Mickäel looks in the mirror at a scrawny upper body and back, a flat chest. The contrast between siblings emphasizes the idea that these two children do not belong in the same gender basket, based on their appearance and behavior. While Mickäel practices spitting, his baby sister, in contrast, practices dancing in a tutu as her "brother" bangs on a toy piano.

The next day, when Mickäel comes to play soccer with the boys, he demonstrates a high degree of skill, eventually taking off his shirt and spitting like the other boys. What follows is a covert urination scene that is typical of many film narratives about transgender people, in a signifier of socially imposed difference and exclusion. As the boys take time out to pee in the grass, Mickäel looks on, puts his shirt back on, and runs into the woods to squat and pee, until he hears his name and the rustle of someone entering the woods. It is unclear whether the younger boy behind him has seen him squatting to urinate, but this scene projects a sense of profound unease and anxiety. Later, back home, he is shown washing his shorts, again casting a critical eye toward the mirror.

While the character defies his assigned gender role, the film defies conventional parental gender stereotypes, particularly during domestic scenes, in which his father seems to be his primary caregiver. When Mickäel plays cards, the father asks if he is cheating, an accusation that points to the notion of deception and Mickäel's feelings of guilt over deceiving his parents. His father is drinking a beer and asks if Mickäel wants to taste it, part of their conspiratorial rule-breaking behavior. The child takes a swig, grimaces lightly, and then rests on his side and sucks his thumb, as if reverting to childhood to avoid the responsibilities and anxieties of adulthood. His father embraces him and says he knows it is not easy to move all the time, confessing to his child that he used to suck his thumb when he was little. He calls him "little monkey," as the scene closes on a nurturing father, rocking his child like a baby in his arms.

In bed, Mickäel gets up, looking in the mirror once again. The next day, while Mickäel is responsible for babysitting Jeanne, the doorbell rings, and Lisa is there, asking, "Why didn't you come?" He answers that he did not want to. Slipping back into the apartment, he decides to leave his sister alone, telling her that he is going out and will come back soon. A shot of her sitting alone cuts to a shot of Lisa dancing in front of Mickäel at her place. "Allez, gosse [Go, boy]!" she teases, as she finally gets him to dance, reluctantly at first. They jitterbug together and mirror each other's movements as the lyrics repeat in English, "I love you." The song ends, and they stand, breathless, looking at each other, as she holds his hand. Then she gets out makeup and puts it on his cheeks and eyes, while he cautions her not to apply too much. She tells him he is pretty as a girl, an ironic statement that he acknowledges in profile, looking at her coyly. When Lisa asks if he knows how to swim, he says yes, but this foretells an activity that will add yet another layer of complication to his impersonation, which will entail wearing a boy's swimsuit. As he makes his way home, hooded, concealing his face, the camera follows from behind as he enters the apartment.

Once inside, tension mounts as Mickäel's mother asks him to come see her, and she notices the makeup, commenting that it looks good. After an embrace from his pregnant mom, he goes to his bedroom and cuts the top off his girl's red swimsuit. Trying it on, he looks at himself in the mirror, turning in profile, chewing his fingernail. While his baby sister works on a puzzle in her bedroom, he solves his own puzzle by making himself a bright-green penis with her clay. Back in his room, he puts on the swimsuit, stuffs the lump of clay in his crotch, and regards himself in the mirror with satisfaction. The next morning, a nerve-wracking scene of roughhousing at the lake prompts viewers to wonder if his prosthetic penis will slip askew or fall out, but no such embarrassing moment occurs. As Mickäel and Lisa walk back home, she holds his hand and leads the way, stopping to kiss him while she holds her hand over his eyes. Slowly he gives a slight grin, returning home and popping his green prosthetic penis into the little box filled with his baby teeth. These moments of humor engage the viewer with Mickäel's project, and the next morning, when Lisa comes to the door and sees his sister, he quickly engages baby sister Jeanne in the deception as well, promising to take her if she keeps quiet. Once she catches onto the game, she joins in with enthusiasm, telling Lisa, "A big brother can defend you," and bragging that Mickäel was the strongest boy in their old community.

A playful neighborhood water fight gives way to an intimate scene in which Mickäel's sister trims his hair, as part of the conspiracy to maintain his gender ruse. Mickäel cautions her not to cut it too short, or their mother will notice. In a ludic scene, he puts on a fake mustache made from the clippings, and so does she, as he talks in a deep voice. This childish gender play emphasizes the central motif and sets up the protagonist for a more serious consequence of masculine conflict the next day. When one of the boys pushes Jeanne, Mickäel is called on to live up to the claim that a brother can defend his sister. He wrestles the boy to the ground, and Lisa looks on admiringly. When the siblings return home, a neighborhood parent knocks on the door to find the "Mickäel" who beat up her child, and the game is up. Like the parents in *Ma Vie en Rose*, Mickäel's mother is humiliated by her child's gender defiance and furiously slaps his face. She makes Mickäel put on a dress over his boy clothing and visit all the neighbors to confess that Mickäel is really a girl named Laure. This scene is particularly painful, and it makes the mother appear cruel, backward, and provincial in her overreaction to the child's masquerade.

After these scenes of humiliation, Mickäel runs into the woods, tears off the dress, leaving only the boy clothing hidden underneath. The camera tilts up into the sky, mirroring the disorientation and visual dislocation of the opening scenes. With a sound of wind or perhaps rain, the camera turns skyward and then down, to reveal Mickäel walking through woods. As he sees his former friends together talking, they start to yell, "Mikael is a girl!" They run after him, and the camera cuts to a shot of them all looking at him, ready to attack. Lisa defends him, saying,

"Stop what are you doing. Leave him," but they reply that if Lisa kissed a girl, "it's disgusting," to which she replies, "Yes, it's disgusting." Lisa leaves Laure crouching at the base of a tree. The next image indicates the passage of time, with the mother holding her new baby, talking about the beginning of school the next day. Laure says she would rather stay home. The next morning, when Laure looks out the balcony, she sees Lisa below and runs downstairs, the sound of footstep echoing as she approaches. The two look at each other for a moment, and then Lisa finally asks, "What's your name?" The closing shot shows the child responding, "Laure," with a slight crooked grin. The *IndieWire* critic Christopher Bell finds fault with this ending:

> It's quite obvious that Laure cannot continue being Mickäel without someone finding out, but the way characters come to terms with this discovery is a bit too easy and Sciamma seems to sweep all of the intricacies of Laure's alter-ego (such as the fact that she has feelings for another female) under the rug. Shouldn't something be said about these issues? Characters swiftly deal with the problem and everyone seems to get over it, and Laure seems to be content with her mother's suggestion that she wear boy clothes but at least admit to being a girl. It's not that the ending can't be positive but we wish greater weight and acknowledgement

had been given to the nuanced issues developed through much of the film. As it stands, "Tomboy" reaches a far too tidy conclusion.

If this ending seems too pat and abrupt, one must remember that, as Roger Ebert declares, "We're not dealing with *Boys Don't Cry* here" (*"Tomboy"*). Instead, the film lands squarely in between, much like the film's star, Zoé Heran. While the film may seem to resolve the issue of gender dysphoria by a socially enforced return to heteronormativity, Zoé's crooked grin also stakes out the possibility of a more open-ended future for Laure and perhaps for Lisa as well.

In contrast to *Tomboy*, a more didactic approach appears in a number of western films, human-interest pieces, reality-television episodes, and series that capitalize on the popular draw of celebrity subjects. These examples tend to exploit viewers' fascination with the more sensational and superficial aspects of transgender experience, as viewers—whether cisgen or transitioning—want to satisfy their curiosity about the details of surgical procedures. *Becoming Chaz* (2011) chronicles the transition process of Chaz (formerly Chastity) Bono, Cher and Sonny Bono's son. One of the most interesting and informative aspects of this film is not the celebrity status of Chaz but the detailed explanation of "bottom surgery."

As the audience watches footage from the Southern Comfort conference session on best options for forming a penis, the film cuts to a side-angle shot of Chaz's face that captures his visible dismay at the alternatives. After watching the presenter discuss the drawbacks of a surgery that has not been perfected thus far, we hear Chaz comment in voice-over, "They haven't really figured out how to make a functioning penis" (York). Toward the close of the film, we see Chaz watching his mother, Cher, being interviewed by David Letterman. Cher misuses pronouns and refers to Chaz as "she," correcting herself and then saying that pronouns do not really matter. Chaz responds to the television set that pronouns do matter, but at least his mother did refer to him as male a few times. In an emotionally effective dialectic, the film cuts back to Cher, who describes how Chaz counsels transgender children who do not want to wear a dress, how people always tell her how brave Chaz is, and how Chaz makes parents more aware of what their children are saying.

Another sort of celebrity from across the Pacific Ocean appears over a decade after *Georgie Girl*, in the New Zealand documentarians Dean Hamer and Joe Wilson's *Kumu Hina* (2014). To understand this traditional indigenous leader, one must consider the vocabulary of gender. The term "transgender" represents a patchwork of meanings, some of which have negative connotations and slang references. Suzanne Woodward explains how the use of transgender as a category arises from Western binary labels, which differ significantly from such non-binary concepts as "the *Hijra* of South Asia, *fa'afafine* of Samoa, *fakaleiti* of Tonga, *mahu* of Hawai'i, *whakawahine* of Aotearoa / New Zealand, *kathoeys* of Thailand, *waria* of Indonesia, *muxe* of Mexico, and the multiple Two-Spirit identities among Native American tribes" (76). She recognizes two films, *Georgie Girl* (Goldson/Wells, 2002) and *Kumu Hina* (Hamer/Wilson, 2014), as outstanding examples of indigenous trans people telling their own stories in a way that fits indigenous cultures and transgender communities.

The New Zealand documentarian Barry Barclay interrogates the practice of the "talking head" first initiated with John Grierson's compilation documentaries, establishing a familiar pattern for many documentarians in the West. Coming from Ngati Apa and Pakeha oral backgrounds, he prioritizes the oratorical *whai kdrero* tradition. A first-person narration on the beliefs and views of an ordinary person is central to this tradition, unlike the omniscient and invisible narrator of films in the style of Grierson and other traditional Western filmmakers. Hina Wong-Kalu speaks about her knowledge of the history of her people in Hawai'i, from the perspective of an indigenous sage and cultural historian. Barclay recommends "talking in," or using indigenous language as a way of making one's own people the primary audience (Woodward 76). At the center of *Kumu Hina* is the repeated word *aloha*, which translates as universal respect and love, including all categories of human beings. When a pupil wants to wear the wreath of flowers, the lei, for both girls and boys, the teacher says, "You get both [lei] because she's both." Woodward observes that "the mode of address shifts easily from the pupil, Ho'onani, to the wider class, highlighting the inseparability of the individual from their [*sic*] broader community" (71).

A central conflict in the film is the tension between Hina's powerful role in the culture and her marriage to a more traditional patriarchal husband, a Fijian named Hema. The film includes scenes of tenderness, but it also displays the tensions that result from Hema being out of his element living in a new country. One of the most disturbing scenes occurs when Hema displays a stereotypically masculine anger and abusive tone when he berates Hina for talking to a man on the telephone. We also see the anxiety Hema feels when Hina must present herself as a woman when they are in Fuji among Hema's friends, who are both transphobic and homophobic and would not accept their relationship otherwise. Hema loves Hina and accepts her *mahu* identity as her real self, but both of them are realistic and aware that not everyone is equally accepting. Their disagreements and fights escalate within the framework of the documentary narrative.

In order to create tension and suspense, the film presents these conflicts as almost insoluble, until Hina makes the decision to take her husband back to visit her friends, especially Kaua'i Iki, who is also *mahu*. In spite of the difficulties, Hina believes that "faith, courage and love will overcome." Conflicts and fights escalate to the point where Hina decides she must take Hema out into the countryside of Hawai'i to return to her own roots and regain her sense of self confidence. Seeing this community seems to work its magic in restoring Hina's sense of self and also on Hema, as he relaxes into a culture that truly practices the often-repeated *aloha* of respect and love. This community has its intended effect on Hema, as demonstrated when the audience sees him picking a birthday present and cake for Hina's birthday. This solicitous attention gives a sense of tender resolution of their conflicts and a maturing of their personal relationship, one that creates more sharing of emotional responsibility and a balance of power and accommodation. The final scene opens out onto a larger narrative as it casts Hina in a realm beyond the domestic and recalls her larger function as a preserver of her culture and its ancient, timeless history. She dances the hula in a dreamy sequence that features the beautiful land of Hawai'i in the background, reminding the viewer of a history much grander and more enduring than the momentary trials of Hina's own personal life.

Joelle Ruby Ryan critiques most documentaries as perpetuating "stereotypes, distortions, biases, and inaccuracies. The media, while not solely or even primarily responsible for cultural and systemic transphobia, is an institution that plays a serious role in the perpetuation of prejudice and discrimination against gender-variant people" (10). Woodward maintains that "as documentaries about high-profile trans people from the Pacific, *Kumu Hina* and *Georgie Girl* display several significant similarities in their celebratory approach of trans identities, framing them as valuable and normal, in direct contrast to the negativity that pervades most Western trans documentaries" (75).

In the more well-known international film adapted from David Ebershoff's fictionalized novel *The Danish Girl* (2000), Tom Hooper's 2015 historical perspective on transgender experience was both popular and controversial for its depiction of one of the first transgender women in Europe. The film opens with scenes of the successful career and happy home life of Einar Wegener (Eddie Redmayne), a Danish landscape artist, and his wife, Gerda Wegener (Alicia Vikander), a lesser-known painter. In steamy bedroom scenes, the film gradually reveals Einar's alter ego, Lili Elbe, the woman Einar says lives inside him. Encouraged by Gerda, Lili emerges and models for Gerda, goes to social events, seeks medical and psychological treatment, and eventually undergoes what is now called gender-confirmation surgery. Although the real-life Elbe was not the first to have such surgery, she leaves us with a personal and detailed account in her diary, *Man into Woman: An Authentic Record of a Change of Sex* (1933).

In a sensationalizing move, the film has full frontal nudity, wherein Redmayne tucks his genitals between his legs and admires a more feminine-looking self in the mirror. Meanwhile, the film omits the real-life annulment of the couple's almost twenty-year marriage. It also avoids the medical details of Lili's death, caused by tissue rejection, depicting instead a romantically quiet death, in which she simply drifts off to a permanent sleep with Gerda at her side. The film resolutely eliminates any of the real-life facts about Gerda's bisexuality, closing with a shot of her and the couple's mutual friend Hans Axgil (Matthias Schoenaerts) high on a hilltop, letting Lili's scarf float off in the wind. Not incidentally, Gerda appears all set to fall into a conventional heterosexual relationship with Hans.

Cáel M. Keegan describes how films such as *Dallas Buyer's Club* (2013), *The Danish Girl* (2015), and *Stonewall* (2015) purport to be progressive but play on the stereotype of gay and trans people as tragic victims: "*The Danish Girl* does little to disabuse viewers of the assumptions that transgender people are tragic and that our bodies are medical anomalies. The film instead passively sanctions these attitudes by removing any historical reference to a theory of why Lili exists, even though European sexologists had developed a robust literature about sex and gender variation by the early twentieth century" (Meyerowitz 15–16).

The strongest critique of mainstream transgender depictions emerges from such scholars as Sarah Schulman, who applies the economic term "disruptive innovation" to the co-opting of gay and trans artistic production. *The Danish Girl* fits this paradigm, primarily in it omissions of historical context:

> Lili never encounters a single person like her, even though the actual Lili most certainly would have. The film suggests that there was absolutely no community available to people like Lili during the 1920s–30s, which is patently false. When the real Lili travelled to Berlin in 1930, the city was a global hub for sex and gender minorities: there were so many people traveling to see Hirschfeld that by 1909 German authorities had begun to issue a special form of identification called a "transvestite pass" (*Transvestitenschien*) to those utilising the institute's services, which included

medical treatment as well as social networking and job placement. The institute treated and politically advocated for high numbers of patients like Lili, estimated minimally at "dozens" before its destruction by the Third Reich in 1933. (Keegan 50)

In spite of the melodramatic exaggerations and lack of historical accuracy or social context of a film such as *The Danish Girl*, it does contribute to a normalization and popularization of transgender stories and histories, and for this reason, it merits inclusion and analysis.

3

NEW PLATFORMS AND
NEW VOICES

The rise of new media and platforms—from Amazon, YouTube, and Hulu to personal blogs, podcasts, and websites—expanded horizons for transgender filmmakers, especially among queer transgender people of color and among women writers and producers.

The filmmaker and media writer Ewan Duarte seeks to create community and recognition among queer transgender people of color (QTPOC), identifying influential figures in independent film. As a filmmaker whose works include *Change over Time* (2013), the story of his own transition from male to female, Duarte reaches out to other transgender filmmakers, including Seyi Adebanjo, Ashley Altadonna, Shaan Dasani, Mikki del Monico, Sam Feder, and Sydney Freeland. Although these filmmakers come from diverse backgrounds, including countries outside the United States, they all speak about their own efforts to capture QTPOC experiences around the world, from Nigeria to a Navajo reservation in New Mexico.

With an MFA in cinema from San Francisco State, Duarte reveals both media expertise and cultural savvy in his work for *IndieWire*, *Huffington Post*, and various film productions. The award-winning *Spiral Transition* (2010) and *Change over Time* were screened in over 140 festivals, including Oslo LGBT Film Festival, Frameline, Melbourne Queer Film Festival, BFI London LGBT Film Festival, DC Shorts Film Festival, Gender DocuFilm Festival in Rome, Hamburg International Queer Film Festival, Rhode Island International Film Festival, and Polari Film Festival in Austin, Texas. His animated experimental film, *Change over Time*, uses an impressionistic style to document Duarte's use of testosterone. Screened in over sixty-five film festivals nationwide and worldwide, it won a Fruitie Award at the Fresh Fruit Festival in New York City. The film incorporates physical changes, interwoven with the director's "inner life and soul changes during [his] first year on 'T'" (Duarte).

Duarte's more recent work includes *Queering Yoga*, which tells stories of transformation and healing with yoga in QTPOC communities, looking at the intersection of LGBTQ identities and "decolonizing" yoga practice. Describing himself and the source of his inspiration, Duarte places gender identity as primary: "I identify as a Trans man (FTM). My identity and my experiences that are aligned to being a Trans man impact all of my creative work" (Duarte). Duarte compares artistic work to the natural cycles of the seasons, noting that change occurs even during a time of rest that is comparable to winter, when the invisible expansion of roots occurs, even though no outward visible growth takes place. He maintains that it is time for trans artists to "rise up and tell [their] own stories" (Duarte), in a collection of interviews offering a theme and variations on important ways to share these stories.

The Nigerian-born Adebanjo expresses a powerful sense of social justice in the short work *Trans Lives Matter! Justice for Islan Nettles*, a documentary first broadcast on PBS Channel 13, through a Brooklyn Museum showing, before screening internationally. As a fellow with the Bronx Museum, Maysles Institute, and City Lore Documentary Institute, to name a few, Adebanjo places spirituality at the center of each film. The documentary *Oya: Something Happened on the Way to West Africa* (2015) received the award for Best Documentary Short at the Baltimore International Black Film Festival. Adebanjo self-describes as gender nonconforming, and his *Oya* makes a case for gender fluidity as part of the Yorùbá culture, tracing roots to the Òrìṣà (African God/dess) tradition of his great-grandmother Chief Moloran Ìyá

Ọlọ́ya. The film is designed to push against recent efforts to outlaw gay marriage and undermine LGBTQ rights in Nigeria, Uganda, Ukraine, Russia, and seventy-five other nations around the world, particularly among people of color.

Adebanjo expresses frustration with those who offer advice from the perspective of a white Western straight person: "I was inundated with solicited and unsolicited opinions and theories," because people "wanted a poverty porn film about Nigeria, the oppression of womyn, trans folks, queers, female genital mutilation, hardships of my family, a first person narrative about my life" (Duarte). This predominantly white impression of Nigerian experience is not the filmmaker's aim, because such a Western perspective undermines the filmmaker's desire to portray subjects with power, humanity, spirituality, and dignity. Adebanjo describes this work as blending media activism with a "passion for social justice and community building": "My work is the intersection of art, media, imagination, ritual and politics. My work is lyrical, engaging people in trans-formative, political and spiritual dialogues" (Duarte). It is interesting to note that throughout Duarte's online interview with Adebanjo, the filmmaker never declares a particular gender, seemingly as an unspoken statement underscoring commitment to gender fluidity.

Across the globe in Milwaukee, Wisconsin, the Houston-born Ashley Altadonna demonstrates her versatility through dynamic and varied media, working as a filmmaker, educator at the award-winning Tool Shed Erotic Boutique, and musician. In addition, she contributes to online publications and Morty Diamond's website, Trans/Love: Radical Sex, Love & Relationships Beyond the Gender Binary. Altadonna established TallLadyPictures.com in 2008, creating an LLC website and blog to make available to distributors such films as *Whatever Suits You* (2007) and *Playing with Gender* (2007). The seven-minute short *Whatever Suits You* presents rapidly changing still images of tailoring a suit, creating a montage that links this process to the experience of trans construction of an externalized gender identity. Altadonna's first feature film, *Making the Cut* (unreleased), documents her Kickstarter fundraising efforts for gender-confirmation surgery, also focusing on "the status of trans health care in America and why certain procedures for transgender folks have often been deemed 'elective or 'cosmetic'" (Duarte). Although the film is a documentary, Altadonna hopes to create a narrative based on her experiences as a trans woman in such a way that "it can inspire other folks" (Duarte). Through her own story, she explains how others manage aspects of production as she trusts specialists to achieve her vision.

Entering a white male-dominated industry as a trans female of color is challenging, but Altadonna views with pride her role as someone whose identities as a trans woman and filmmaker are "irrevocably entwined." Like Adebanjo, she hopes her life experiences will provide a sense of community for those who "are POC or queer" (Duarte). She delivers this inspiration in various ways, from the almost art-house style of *Whatever Suits You* to the mock-documentary style of *Playing with Gender*, perhaps an homage to Ann Pelo's earlier article of the same name, a study in which educators record the gender-fluid preschool activities and comments of preschoolers at Seattle Hilltop Child Care Center. In this article, one girl declares, "I hate princesses; that's why I'm a boy" (Pelo).

Coming out of Chapman University's MFA program in film, Shaan Dasani has experience as an actor and award-winning filmmaker with more than thirty short pieces under his direction. In his first major acting role in Blank Theater's production of Michael A. Shepperd's *The Not Lesbians*, Dasani plays Ollie, a young man seeing his ex-girlfriend for the first time after his transition. After playing Kate in Queer Classic's performance of Shakespeare's *The Taming of the Shrew*, directed by Casey Kringlen, Dasani was in the first web advertisement for Google Goals and went on to act in *Porno Dido*, at the Hollywood

Fringe Festival (2016). He developed Karma Theory film company for small projects, ads, web design, music videos, a digital reality series, and narrative features. He speaks with students about his transition and filmmaking experience, including how he created a short web film with minimal equipment, shot on a cell phone and laptop camera, edited with Final Cut 7 and stock free music from the web (Duarte).

Dasani takes a critical view of his own work, describing how he held himself back initially after "a lifetime of playing it safe in [his] real life" (Duarte). Dasani explains the process:

> I always had carried myself as "tomboy," but there was some part of me that was wanting to assimilate into this role of daughter/sister/niece/girl even though I didn't feel like that. I didn't want to stick out, I wanted to blend in. Even being a South Asian person who grew up in the American south—I wanted to feel like I was like everyone else. And so while I'm very proud of my work, I now feel like something has been lifted, I'm not hiding anymore. The thing is, they say transition is a process, and that's true. It's not like, now that I've transitioned all my work will be deep and meaningful and inspiring. It's that a huge step was taken in my real life to not hide, and it encourages me to keep finding places of fear in my work and push past those places for a

more authentic experience in the art, whether that's acting or filmmaking. (Duarte)

For whatever reason, Dasani describes his shift from female to male as relatively smooth. Because MTF public identity represents a step down in the social hierarchy, whereas FTM carries more prestige in a patriarchal culture, the difficulties for trans women may reflect—at least to some degree—the hardship of taking on a less socially powerful gender category.

Unlike the mixed experience that some trans women describe, Dasani states that his transition from female to male was "a positive experience overall," although he adds, "Being a transman is not my only identity. Not all projects I do have to be about transition and not all characters I play have to be transmen." As a filmmaker and actor, Dasani wants to create "more honest stories and characters, so that the audience, whatever their own personal experiences, can relate" (Duarte). Dasani's on-camera credits include CBS's *Criminal Minds: Beyond Borders*, along with directing music videos for Antigone Rising, a female alt-band, and commercials produced and filmed for Wells Fargo and Google. Dasani speaks of living an authentic life, and this bold expression of selfhood has garnered the Alfred P. Sloan Screenwriting Award and Feature Film Production Grant.

Working in Los Angeles, Mikki del Monico describes how his work and personal evolution intertwine, a sentiment echoed by a number of other transgender artists of color. His debut work, *Alto* (2015), garnered the "audience favorite" award for a feature-film debut and the best first-time director award at the Downtown Film Festival Los Angeles. *Alto* is a comedy that incorporates Italian and Mafia references, family, and transgender identity. Del Monico describes finding his voice and expanding outside his comfort zone: "I was writing myself into exposure. . . . The path to making this film involved my coming out to my family as transgender. I was fortunate that when I leapt, they opened their arms" (Duarte).

Del Monico's wide-ranging background includes work beyond film as a personal trainer, feature scriptwriter, short-form storyteller, and digital technician on a cruise ship. Nodding to the stunning variety of his experience, he comments on the path that took him to life as a trans male, "As much as this journey has shaped the man I am, I never want it to be the most interesting thing about me" (Duarte). Del Monico's latest work includes adapting the film version of *Alto* into a musical format. Like Dasani, Del Monico's trans identity "often takes a back seat to a lot of other facets." He observes, "When I decided to become a filmmaker, I was actually saying, yes, I can handle rejection, disappointment, criticism, and naysayers, and I can do so in a way that brings something valuable to the world. I was saying the same thing when I came out as transgender" (Duarte). Those included in Duarte's list of "filmmakers to watch" all emphasize the supreme importance of community for TQPOC artists.

As with Duarte and other transgender filmmakers, Sam Feder asserts the need for transgender voices and creative autonomy in film art. Working in both New York and Los Angeles, Feder is not afraid to wade into controversial territory among members of the LGBTQ community. He proved this with his best known film, *Kate Bornstein Is a Queer and Pleasant Danger* (2014), which follows the famous male-to-female trans celebrity who prompted a blunt description in the *Village Voice*: "Author of the 1994 book *Gender Outlaw* and a veteran performance artist of her own shows, such as *Hidden: A Gender*, Bornstein has managed to both anger and delight most camps in the LGBTQ universe" (Ortega). Feder's subject is described as a "a transsexual, Jewish, lesbian, bipolar, masochistic cutter," who has offended individuals from almost every category in a complex and loosely knit community (Ortega). Premiering at the British Film Institute, Feder's film won multiple awards in 2014, but not without controversy, as befits the film's subject. Instead of taking a traditional biopic approach to his subject, which tends to idealize the subject, Feder explores the gamut of

Bornstein's attitudes, including aspects of her life that may alienate some viewers, as he notes: "There is so much to explore with Kate—gender, sexuality, SM, performance, writing, public vs. private, mental illness, suicide, Scientology, loss of family, creation of queer family. While touching on all of that, the film reflects Kate's idiosyncratic, brilliant and rebellious nature" (Ortega). His talent in producing such sophisticated and nuanced work has earned a wide range of accolades and grants from such prestigious organizations as the John D. and Catherine T. MacArthur Foundation, the Jerome Foundation, Astraea Foundation for Social Justice Crossroads Foundation, and the Ellen Stone Belic Institute for the Study of Gender in the Arts and Media (Ortega).

Feder and Julie Hollar's first feature, *Boy I Am* (2006), was streamed for free through Women Make Movies, in response to attacks on transgender individuals. Feder believes it is essential for trans artists to tell their own stories, and he acknowledges that in spite of challenges, he looks to the past for inspiration to tackle issues of social justice and visibility for trans people of color: "I'm a huge fan of *The Celluloid Closet*, *Ethnic Notions*, and *Color Adjustment*. For years I've wanted to see a documentary like those focused on trans people, but I didn't have the resources" (Duarte). He points to the example of Marley Dias, an eleven-year-old who collected and donated one thousand books featuring a black female protagonist, quoting Marian Wright Edelman's saying, "You can't be what you can't see" (Jong). In spite of—or perhaps because of—the controversy surrounding some of his work, he closes one interview with this advice: "Build community with your peers (help each other!)—don't fall victim to fears of scarcity. And be kind" (Duarte).

Sydney Freeland began her career with encouragement in the form of fellowships from Sundance Native Lab, Ford Foundation, Time Warner, and a Fulbright Scholarship (2005). Her first independent feature, *Drunktown's Finest* (2014), was screened at Sundance, winning a Grand Jury Prize and also receiving an Outstanding First Feature Award from HBO at Outfest in Los Angeles and a nomination for outstanding feature from GLAAD Media Awards. She grew up in New Mexico on a Navajo reservation, frustrated because she never saw people like herself represented in media. Inspired by the Coen brothers' comedy *Raising Arizona* (1987), her current work is a "dark comedy" about characters named Deidra and Laney Rob a Train. Moving from writing to directing with the new-media series *Her Story*, Freeland was thrilled to have the opportunity to direct: "I remember reading the script and thinking 'Wow, I didn't even know I wanted this.' I really liked that it was a story about Trans women, but it wasn't about transition. It's been over 10 years since

I transitioned and I felt like I could relate to Jen and Laura's script on personal level" (Duarte). Although she faced some challenges, with no "frame of reference," she remarks that "there has been this monumental shift in the past couple years with shows like *Transparent* and people like Laverne Cox and Caitlyn Jenner becoming household names" (Duarte).

In another platform, Caitlin Jenner is the most famous recent example of MTF transition, shocking audiences fixated on the masculinity and physical prowess of her former identity as a famous male Olympic athlete. Once Bruce transitioned to become Caitlin, the focus shifted to aspects that people often associate with female identity. The public was soon fascinated by clothing, makeup, and surgical procedures, but in an interview with Ellen DeGeneres, Caitlin returns to the memory of what life was like before she transitioned. She reveals that her wife knew about her desire to be a woman ("Ellen"). There is a certain irony in watching DeGeneres, dressed in low-key masculine dress, interacting with the perfectly coiffed and traditionally adorned Caitlin Jenner. The economic aspects of Jenner's transition drew attention and some criticism, with a number of people observing that a wealthy person can afford to have the surgeries but most ordinary people cannot. In addition, some feminists pointed out the irony that the first sixty-year-old woman to grace the cover of *Vanity Fair* was born a man.

Another transgender production affected by the intersection of celebrity, gender, and social class is the successful web-based series *Transparent*, which falls into some traps that Keegan identifies in his critique of *The Danish Girl* but manages to avoid others. For example, Keegan notes that *The Danish Girl* creates a false history in order to establish the character's loneliness and uniqueness. On the other hand, *Transparent*, based on a fictional character named Mort/Maura Pfefferman (Jeffrey Tambor), goes out of its way to present a character who is supported by a well-meaning family and community. Every family member except the central character's wife, Shelly (Judith Light), is initially somewhat shocked, but they rapidly become accepting and as supportive as a family of egoists can be. Its premise is based on the path of a divorced father of four beginning the process of transitioning from male to female.

Maura serves as both family glue and yeast, holding the family together and causing it to grow and transform. Indeed, as the characters unfold, the audience realizes that practically every family member has sexual secrets that Maura's example inspires them to reveal. Far from exoticizing trans experience, the series normalizes and humanizes the central character. Although some trans critics question the casting choice—as is appropriate and understandable—one may also argue that Jeffrey Tambor's reputation and accretion of previous roles actually help mainstream audiences identify with Maura as an old friend who has been carrying a lonely secret. The series encourages viewers to celebrate her decision and accept it as revealing the real self behind the gender-restrictive social mask.

In American culture, television and film have an outsized influence on people's understanding and formulation of happiness, particularly in the realm of gender roles. Although some observers credit the recent Supreme Court ruling in favor of gay marriage for the sea change in public attitudes toward the LGBQT community, others argue that the decision merely reflects a cultural shift that has been occurring over the past couple of decades. Some go a step further and attribute this change to the influence of popular television series such as *Will and Grace* and, more recently, *Glee, Grey's Anatomy, True Blood, Orange Is the New Black*, and the Amazon series *Transparent*—all of which present LGBQT characters in a sympathetic light. *Transparent* is unprecedented in its popularity and critical acclaim, winning six Emmys and the Golden Globe Award for Best Television Series. Through innovative web distribution on Amazon, creator Jill Soloway's vision of the series narrative as a "wounded father being replaced by a blossoming femininity" capitalized on a dominant motif in recent American culture, using its advertising as a comedy to draw the maximum range of viewers.

Although some people criticize the series for casting a cisgender male in the role rather than a trans woman, Soloway has her reasons for casting Tambor. If she had chosen a transgender woman, it would have required a more documentary approach, finding a trans woman who had done no hormonal or emotional transitioning. Tambor is a recognizable actor, known for his work in several popular series, particularly as a touchy sycophant sidekick, Hank, in *The Larry Sanders Show* and as both George Bluth and his twin, Oscar, in *Arrested Development*. Tambor was almost legendary for being nominated but not winning Emmy Awards for best actor in a comedy series, but his near-miss streak was broken in 2015 when he won thirteen best actor awards for his performance in *Transparent*. This series turned out to be one of the most popular and critically acclaimed contenders across the board in a growing field of web-accessed series, in 2015 and 2016 winning Emmy, Golden Globe, British Academy of Television, and Screen Actors Guild awards for best lead actor, series, director, writer, producer, and best foreign television, among its many awards. This record is relevant because it indicates not only how successful the marketing was but also how effective Soloway was in creating a narrative that appealed to a wide swath of viewers by diversifying its plotline and point of view. If the central focus of a transitioning trans woman is at the heart of its appeal, the screenplay and camera glide through the lives of a sprawling family in a way that immediately engages viewers' curiosity and sympathy for every character. As Tambor's Mort decides to become a woman in order to thrive emotionally, the director and screenwriters make narrative and casting choices that ensure the survival of their product, providing fantasy solutions to problems of social alienation, rejection, and economic competition.

Narratives that depict affluent characters in first-world settings as the unspoken social background allow free choices in matters of gender, but these are often not available to people in lower socioeconomic categories. In tandem with the blossoming popularity of androgynous figures in American film and television entertainment, sociologists and psychologists have devoted increasing study to gender dysphoria, absent fathers, working mothers, and the psychological ramifications of a culture steeped in macho values. With the prevalence of stereotypically masculine entertainments comes the common habit of equating financial success or physical domination with happiness. One aim in analyzing *Transparent*'s success is to expose connections between the popular appeal of ambiguously gendered central characters in film and television and the concurrence of larger social movements toward female and transgender empowerment, particularly in the face of a national and international climate that continues to downplay everything from social entrapment of women and date rape on college campuses to female abduction, sex slavery, hate crimes against gays and transgender people, and honor killings abroad and in the United States. In contrast to this brutal reality—in the true spirit of capitalism—films with happy endings usually involve spending and/or receiving money.

Transparent's opening credits create a pastiche of nostalgic family images, mingled with the faces of famous drag queens and a tantalizing set of fragments from popular culture of the past four decades. Although advance publicity prepares viewers for the secret of Maura's trans identity, the narrative skips between the present moment and key scenes from the past to reveal that every member of the family has a number of hidden secrets, mostly sexual. The editing of the series interweaves the complex lives of family members, relations, and friends in a way that gives each one an authentic backstory, creating elements of mystery, curiosity, sympathy, and almost slapstick humor. Cross-cutting and flashbacks illustrate the hidden sexual lives of characters, even as Mort's transition to become Maura is the background against which all family members relive and experience their own transitions. Jeffrey Tambor's depiction of Maura inspires occasional laughter, but moments of courage and frank expression of who she is catch the viewer by surprise with a sudden welling of emotion and identification. After the eldest daughter, Sarah (Amy Landecker), first discovers Mort dressed as a woman, Maura says, "We need to talk." As Maura's secrets unfold, Sarah asks if Maura has been dressing as a woman in secret all her life. With a simple dignity and tenderness, Maura answers, "No, honey, I've been dressing up as a man all my life. This is who I am." The quiet force and authenticity with which Tambor delivers these lines are a testament to the actor's powers.

As a backdrop, the silent star of *Transparent* is the beautiful family home in the Palisades, purchased for $80,000 in the 1970s and now pushing $5, $10, or $15 million dollars in resale value. The issue of selling the house serves as a constant drumbeat, with each family member creating a secret arrangement with the father, who cautions them not to talk to their siblings about their agreements. These patterns of deception, hidden sacrifices, and keeping secrets among the siblings are typical of many families, and as Maura observes, "Everything we do, no one sees it." The viewer gets glimpses into all of the moments no one else sees in flashbacks: Josh, molested by his babysitter, growing up and having sex with underage girls yet returning to his babysitter even as an adult; Mort reveling in his femininity the first time when he goes to Camp Camellia, for cross-dressers; thirteen-year-old Alexandra (Abby Hoffman) wandering off to drink beer and kiss an older boy at the beach, then confessing that she is not seventeen but thirteen. The sequence closes with the camera zooming into her open mouth, as if the audience is probing the interior of her being.

In contrast to many real-life transgender individuals, Maura's family is reasonably accepting of her new identity. In part, their blasé attitude seems to stem from their self-centeredness and self-absorption, characteristics revealed when they attend the LGBQT support group's talent show. Maura conquers her fears and performs, wearing a glamorous dress and singing while her family bickers in the audience. Their rude, distracted behavior and early departures illustrate how hard it is to gain family support, even among those who accept—at least superficially—the choice to transition to a new identity or simply to unveil an old identity long hidden. Each season closes with an ending of at least one phase in the family's communal life. Near the end of the first season, Soloway's narrative focuses on the death of Shelly's second husband, who was shown wandering off and getting lost in earlier humorous vignettes. In the final episode, he lies silent, bedridden in the background, as Maura and

Shelly discuss this final transition and rediscover the love that brought them together when Maura was Mort.

As fictional television series entertain and perhaps educate adults about adult transgender lives, other filmmakers tackle the issue by looking primarily at the other end of the age and genre spectrum, through documentary profiles. The economic backdrop of television coverage is muted in comparison to discussions of economics in documentaries. The chief anxiety of most transitioning individuals is the cost of these expensive and complicated surgical procedures. Considering this looming burden and barrier, other stories of social persecution, ostracism, and even occasional physical violence seem minor in comparison to the financial cost, but news stories rarely discuss money, instead focusing on a human-interest format. In one series, NBC makes little pretense of impartiality, stating that "from the White House rolling back guidance to protect transgender kids in school to the Supreme Court announcing it will no longer hear the case of trans student Gavin Grimm, it has been a disheartening past few weeks for supporters of transgender rights." The portrait's goal is "putting faces to those who will be impacted by these decisions" (McCarthy). Like web-based fictional series, these short pieces shape the consciousness of the public at large.

Growing Up Coy (2016) tells the story of six-year-old Coy Mathis, whose Colorado public grade school would not let her use the girls' restroom. Her parents sought out Michael Silverman, once part of the Transgender Legal Defense and Education Fund, to file a civil rights lawsuit. Once the family became the subject of media attention, Eric Juhola and Jeremy Stulberg began filming their fight, maintaining a sympathetic and restrained stance as they filmed the family's struggle to maintain the rights and privacy of their child and still tell her story. This example poses a difficult dilemma surrounding privacy and agency, given Coy's age and the parents' position as the arbiters of her fate. Once the school made this decision, however, the family did not have much choice in spreading her story, since it became common knowledge as the subject of local and eventually state and national news. Once her case became news, supporters contributed to her cause and offered various kinds of support to the beleaguered family. The technique of the filmmakers was to offer a platform to work through issues and process emotions as the family struggled to help Coy find a supportive educational and social environment. The short film does not gloss over her problems, but it offers hope, insight, and inspiration to transgender youth and their families as they face and surmount similar challenges.

Dante Alencastre directs *Raising Zoey* (2016), the story of Zoey Luna, a trans teen whose mother helps her overcome bullying in middle school in California. Zoey decides to take an active role in publicizing the discrimination as she struggles for acceptance in her California middle school, where she was alienated and bullied. Alencastre's intimate piece shows Zoey fighting ostracism and calling for visibility, as she becomes more and more active in speaking out about the kinds of discrimination she has confronted. Becoming an activist has allowed Zoey to become a role model for others facing ostracism, and her role has allowed her to express her own sense of satisfaction since she transitioned. One scene features Zoey's mother speaking at a rally, calling on people to "keep our children safe. Let's accept them and love them for who they are."

In contrast to Coy's and Dante's experiences, *Real Boy* (2016) looks at a family that is not unified in its response to the isolation and fear experienced by transgender young people. The documentary features the nineteen-year-old musician Bennett Wallace, who looks outside the family to the successful trans musician Joe Stevens for encouragement and guidance. Shaleece Haas's documentary portrait reveals how Bennett's mother expresses anxiety and uncertainty about his choice to fully transition. Faced with his mother's resistance, Bennett represents one of the many trans individuals who creates his own nonbiological family and support system as he shapes and grows into his newly established public identity.

In "Becoming More Visible," *NBC Nightly News* presented a series of pieces on transgender children, including "Growing Up Transgender: Malisa's Story." This one is notable because Malisa's grandfather is the congressman Mike Honda, who makes his story public in order to encourage other families in similar circumstances. Malisa describes the first time she saw herself with a wig: "I saw the person who I really was." The eight-year-old explains her transition, saying her parents "didn't understand at first, but then they did." The YouTube video receives a variety of responses; most are supportive, but a few are from people who declare that parents should simply force children into gender conformity with their birth assignment.

"Meet the Transgender NCAA Swimmer from Harvard" features Schuyler Bailar, a swimmer who transitioned from female to male in high school (Olympic). This film takes viewers through a gamut of emotions in its brief thirteen and a half minutes, flashing back to footage of Bailar as a self-proclaimed "tomboy" who wore cargo pants, swam, and performed rollerblade jumps. Bailar's path to a transition was sometimes rocky, but he was lucky to have parents who fully supported him throughout a complicated process. What begins as a fairly lighthearted telling of his story suddenly turns serious when he takes the final step of revealing to his Korean grandmother his decision to transition. Much to his relief, her only concern is that it is the role of a Korean daughter to take care of her mother and that he will no longer be a daughter. When she asks if he will still promise to care for his mother all his life, he tells her that he can handle this. He tattoos this promise, written in her handwriting next to his heart, under the scar from his breast-reduction surgery.

In transitioning to male, Bailar also faces the prospect of losing his spot as a top female athlete to become a male swimmer, a decision made all the more challenging when he breaks his back. After a period of depression and uncertainty, he returns to the pool and makes the men's swim team at Harvard, becoming the first openly transgender athlete to compete in NCAA events. As a motivational speaker, he describes his journey in order to help other transgender youth conquer obstacles and achieve happiness and a true sense of identity. The piece closes with his declaration, "If I can be naked in a Speedo and expose my trans-ness to everybody, you can do your thing too." Two elements in this compelling documentary somewhat complicate its upbeat message. Bailar's family and educational background signal a level of wealth that not all transgender individuals enjoy, and his transition as

a competitive athlete from female to male does not carry
the complications often involved in this domain. Austin
Johnson takes a sociological approach to documentaries
on MTF people, looking at the following films to identify narrative patterns: *You Don't Know Dick: Courageous
Hearts of Transsexual Men* (1997); *Southern Comfort*
(2001); *Call Me Malcolm* (2005); *Transparent* (2005);
Transgender Revolution (2006); *Enough Man* (2006); *Still
Black: A Portrait of Black Transmen* (2008); and *Becoming
Chaz*. He identifies two consistent motifs that emphasize
medical terminology and a "discovery narrative" (468).
The idea of inhabiting a "wrong body" is another common feature of such trans documentaries (476), and this
negative language imagery and medicalization of the trans
body dictates medical as the required course for "the actu-
alization of transgender identity" (475).

In addition, this model dovetails with the commercial,
medical, and social regulatory system dominant in late
twentieth- and early twenty-first-century Western societies. Johnson also notes incidentally that one of the issues
that affects people's choice of a medical intervention is the
common custom of housing people in school, military,
prison, and other institutional settings "according to their
legal and thus genitalia-based sex. In order to be housed
according to their personal and authentic sex identification, transgender people must be legally classified as

such" (470). Qualifying for this legal category usually requires proof of medical assessments, procedures, and treatments. Johnson also observes in closing that people of color are much more likely to find it financially challenging to "solve" their problematic body issues. The high cost of medical interventions perpetuates further marginalization of trans people of color, who are more likely to live below the poverty line than white populations are. Johnson does not mention a statistical correlation that places people of color disproportionately in such gender-segregated settings, especially prison and the military, but this certainly exacerbates the problem.

The most fascinating aspect of this study is the consistency of the language and sentiments of the subjects in these films. Johnson does not try to naturalize their comments by assuming some essentialist foundation for transgender expression, nor does he try to argue, on the other hand, that this language is prompted or encouraged by social factors and medical establishments that influence people's way of viewing transgender people's lived experiences. He does arrange the responses in chronological order, perhaps to suggest or identify the various stages in developing awareness as MTF perceive their dilemma. In *Still Black: Portrait of Black Transmen*, Ethan recalls early childhood experiences: "I remember asking my father when I was about three years old when my penis was gonna grow and it totally freaked him out. But I knew, I mean, I would see little boys and I always wanted to hang out with them all the time" (Johnson 477).

Jules Rosskam's documentary *Transparent* (2004) documents nineteen female-to-male transsexuals who have borne and raised biological children. One subject describes a moment from a later period in life: "I do remember when I was about, like, eight years old, and I went into this grocery store, and I, for some reason—I don't even know what the conversation was—but I stood up, and I said, 'You know, when I grow up, I'm gonna be a man.'" In *Enough Man* (2006), Wendel does not go so far as to compare female characteristics to cancer, but he does describe a similarly negative emotional response to the feeling of having breasts: "I feel like there's this thing between my chest and my partners. And that is really hard for me because like no matter how someone touches it, they're not going to be able to touch what really feels like it's a part of me. I'm really looking forward to being touched after surgery and, like, how good that's going to feel" (Johnson 481). Johnson concludes that, in the works analyzed, "the privileging of narratives regarding child-hood and adolescent identification with maleness and disdain for femaleness is common throughout the films" (485). He adds that "in featuring narratives of desire for a body that is congruent with male identification and social presentation of gender, the films promote the need for medical interventions" (485). This anodyne sociological statement makes no value judgment, but a number of connotations may be unpacked by deconstructing these responses from a more value-based or less scientific perspective. Marxist critics or people who are skeptical about the medicalization of gender may see this perceived "need" as a manufactured or profit-driven solution to an emotional state. Some feminist scholars may view this pattern as a typical result or attitude of a society that devalues the feminine and glamorizes or privileges masculine physical and emotional traits.

The documentary *Transgender Revolution* (2007) tackles the next phase of responses to body dysphoria, finding a medical "solution" to the perceived problem, which the subject, Terry, compares to "having cancer." Johnson describes Terry's description as "a narrative justifying his decision to spend thirty thousand dollars on transition related surgeries": "It's not elective. It's not a choice. You're not happy with yourself. You can't hardly stand yourself physically.... Being transsexual is no different to me than like having cancer. You have to have it removed. You have to have it taken care of. You can't just live with it. Eventually it will eat you alive, just like cancer" (Johnson 480, 477). The topic of cost recurs in documentaries with subjects who see sexual traits as a form of illness.

In Joseph Parlagreco's *Call Me Malcolm* (2010), Malcolm Himschoot expresses more of an ongoing sense of emotional invisibility and isolation: "When I was a kid, I used to think of myself as one of the brothers. I have two brothers so that would have made me the third brother but other people perceived me as a girl. And I couldn't really correct them. It made me feel like I wasn't there" (Johnson 478). In *Becoming Chaz*, Bono discusses an even later perception and stronger negative emotions surrounding his lack of preparedness for puberty and his sense of genuine alarm: "When I went through puberty it was obvious. Like, oh fuck, what's happening?! In high school often at night I would go to bed praying I would wake up the next day as a boy" (Johnson 478).

The same feelings of longing and urgency emerge in fictional narratives. Sophie Hyde's *52 Tuesdays* (2013) harks back to Sally Potter's playful depiction of passing time in *Orlando*, creatively structured through snapshots of fifty-two weeks of gender transition. Like many of the international works discussed in this volume, this Australian film presents an initial degree of mystery and disorientation. It opens with the central character, teenaged Billie (Tilda Cobham-Hervey), talking into the camera in a darkened closet: "I used to have a mom who told me everything." The audience soon learns that this is no longer true, if it ever was the case. Billie goes to live with her estranged father, Tom (Beau Travis Williams), in order to allow her mother, Jane (Del Herbert-Jane), to transition into being her father, James. One hears a sense of irony in her voice as she muses on her past relationship with her mother: "In my family, we made decisions together. I felt like an adult."

A quick flashback reveals the rather brutal way Billie learns of her mother's secret life. We see a close-up in the mirror of Jane squashing and binding rather large breasts, and then the shot tilts up to reveal the face of what appears to be a man with a goatee. A knock on the door forces the confrontation between Billie and her mother, Jane, who emerges as James (Del Herbert-Jane). They talk awkwardly and finally agree that Billie will move in with her father for a while and visit once a week. Over the course of a year, the narrative includes vignettes of Billie seeing a psychiatrist with James, eating at a restaurant, and mostly arguing. In a self-reflexive nod to the power of filmmaking, every Tuesday is depicted with the androgynous teenaged girl talking into her video camera. This structure is interspersed with the date of each visit and brief clips of news stories that occur on that date. This added touch gives viewers a snapshot of events occurring out in the big world, contrasted with self-absorbed characters who feel as if their personal worlds are disintegrating before their eyes. Without being heavy-handed, this device positions the personal narrative in history and suggests that people's emotional struggles take place against a background of larger conflicts that affect the human race and the planet as a whole.

The film reveals tense moments of conflict, as Billie has a difficult time accepting the sudden changes in her life. The narrative ventures fearlessly into scenes depicting teenage sexuality, which gives a controversial edge to the film. At school, Billie peeks in a costume room and witnesses a boy and girl having sex, and when the girl notices Billie, the two simply look at each other while Billie continues to watch. Billie then befriends the couple, Jasmin (Imogen Archer) and Josh (Sam Althuizen), and convinces her uncle Harry (Mario Späte) to loan her the key to a warehouse where they can meet. Billie videotapes the couple, asking what it is like to have sex, eventually taping them while they perform various sex acts. Meanwhile, James begins an affair with Lisa (Danica Moors), which he conceals from Billie, all the while remaining oblivious to Billie's activities.

The filmmaker refuses to portray an easy path to transition, picking out possible roadblocks to place in the narrative. For example, when James tries to use testosterone, it only works for a short while before he learns that he has a rare reaction that causes him to overproduce liver enzymes. James sinks into depression, and Billie finds him drunk, whereupon she takes a swig from the bottle herself. Billie says in voice-over, "I was always praised for my sophistication, my maturity, but it was never true." This is nowhere more evident than in her inability to understand the seriousness of videotaping sex acts among juveniles. When the parents receive a call from the principal about Billie texting a nude photo to another girl during class time, the school alerts the parents that this constitutes the crime of child pornography. The principal says it must be difficult for "a family like yours," but James says the family has given Billie "a good perspective that equipped [her] with better understanding." The audience sees the irony in this statement exposed when James must visit a psychiatrist with Billie in order to qualify for top surgery. When James says, "Despite the hiccup, things are pretty good," Billie replies, "Yeah. Outside of that, I've been lying about mom. I've been going around fucking around without anyone knowing where I am. Hasn't known until just now. Really fucking good, isn't it? James has been seeing someone from work, but I don't have any fucking idea."

The final turning point occurs when Billie's biological father has an accident, and the whole family ends up together at the hospital, where he delivers a heartfelt speech to her: "Most people do things with the best intentions. Things just don't work out. That's life, Bill. You don't want what you had before, knowing only a few pieces of someone. You have a chance to know who your mother really is, and that's when you make the choice to love him or not." In the final scene, Billie returns to live with James. She looks at her watch as it turns over to the date exactly a year from when she moved out of her childhood home. This work conveys all the complexity and struggle of adolescence for the child of a parent who transitions, but it closes with a sense of emotional evolution for all the characters. It refuses to offer complete closure, but it proffers a note of hope and optimism for a family that seems authentic and complete.

In the hybrid genre of biopics, the Australian made-for-television *Carlotta* (2014) presents the life of Carlotta, a transgender woman who ran off to Sydney in 1965 to join and become the star of Les Girls drag show. The show took off when Australia's Channel 9 broadcast an interview with Carlotta from the dressing room, and the cabaret act soon became a draw for tourists. Carlotta went on to be the first trans actor to play a trans character in 1973, in the soap opera *Number 96*, using the pseudonym Carolle Lea. A writer for *A Gender Variance Who's Who* comments, "It is ironic that Carlotta, who pioneered trans playing trans in 1973, is portrayed by a cis actor in the 2014 biography" ("Carlotta"). Glenn Dunks concedes some value in the production's ability to convey an authentic emotional tone: "David Hannam's screenplay may not do anything with the transgender pioneer's life that isn't in the standard biopic playbook, and a cisgender actor, Jessica Marais, may have been cast as Carlotta both before and after transition, but the telemovie does manage to hit the right dramatic notes" (28). Dunks claims that Carlotta helped inspire *Priscilla, Queen of the Desert*, and she went on to perform as a panelist for the television program *Beauty and the Beast*, continuing to tour Australia into the new millennium.

The second decade of the new millennium witnessed a sea change in attitudes toward transgender artists, underscored by the emergence of more mainstream artists publicly declaring their transgender identity. The Wachowski brothers took turns acknowledging their gender status, first Lana (born as Laurence Wachowski in 1965), who transitioned in 2008, and then Lilly (born as Andrew Paul Wachowski in 1967), who transitioned later in 2016. Famous for their work on *Bound* (1996), *The Matrix* franchise (1999, 2003), production of *V for Vendetta* (2006), and the television series *Sense8* (2017), these filmmakers do not feature transgender issues as a central theme. Preferring to keep their lives private, they both went public as women in order to offer inspiration and courage to others who have kept their true identity a secret from the world. They also publicly encourage viewers and critics to reread thematic elements in their earlier works to glean elements that reflect their attitudes and perceptions about the true nature of individual identity.

The Academy Awards for 2018 were groundbreaking in delivering the first nomination to a transgender director, Yance Ford, for *Strong Island* (2017), a documentary about the slaying of his brother. Because it is a nomination in a major category, this has captured public attention, but it is not without precedent. Previous trans nominees in other categories include Anohni for the song "Manta Ray" in *Racing Extinction* (2015), Paige Warner for visual effects in a system to capture facial performance, and Angela Morley for the score of *The Slipper and the Rose: The Story of Cinderella and the Little Prince* (Dubowsky 125).

One of the latest critically acclaimed fictional works is the Chilean Sebastián Lelio's *A Fantastic Woman* (2017, *Una mujer fantástica*), which received the first Oscar for a best foreign picture featuring both a transgender central character and actor. It is the story of two lovers—Marina (Daniela Vega), an aspiring young entertainer who works as a waitress, and Orlando (Francisco Reyes), a successful printing-company owner who is twenty years older. In the midst of Orlando's birthday celebration at their apartment, he suddenly collapses, and Marina must get him to the hospital as quickly as possible. Soon after their arrival at the emergency room, Orlando, dies and Marina finds herself immediately under suspicion, partly because of her youth but also because everyone suspects that she is a gold-digger and possibly worse. The hospital staff keeps her from seeing her lover's body, and the family even suspects some sort of foul play; so they have her investigated.

The *New York Times* critic A. O. Scott describes the progression of the film from realist melodrama to surreal morality tale: "Later, her daily routines—and Mr. Lelio's adherence to the conventions of realism—will be disrupted by moments of fantastical spectacle and surreality. And in the course of a series of ordeals that begins with Orlando's death, many of the people Marina encounters will question whether she's really a woman at all." Police and hospital staff use male pronouns to refer to Marina, and eventually a female detective confirms that Marina—in addition to being young and poor—is transgender. Orlando's former wife (Aline Kuppenheim) will not allow her to attend his funeral, and his son (Nicolás Saavedra) vows to evict her from the apartment the couple shared; he even takes the dog away from Marina. Orlando's ex-wife and other family members see Marina as an imposter and a perverse fraud, considering the relationship unnatural. Undaunted, Marina refuses to be cowed by the family, and she maintains her own sense of identity, proving herself to be the "fantastic woman" of the title. This phrase conveys two senses of the word "fantastic," the first being unbelievable or strange and the second being unparalleled and formidable. By the end of the narrative, she lives up to the more favorable version by remaining direct and bold, steadfast in her memory of Orlando and their love.

This film achieved critical acclaim, with a host of awards, including the Academy Award for Best Foreign Language Film of 2017. Scott gives the film the ultimate praise by comparing the director and his creation to avant-garde film greats: "Almodóvarian and Buñuelian grace notes adorn its matter-of-fact melody, and its surface modesty camouflages an unruly, extravagant spirit. You may not realize until the very end that you have been gazing at the portrait of an artist in the throes of self-creation." The critic's comparison is well deserved for an innovative film and subtle performance that captures the zeitgeist of our era.

CONCLUSION

One might apply A. O. Scott's phrase "portrait of an artist in the throes of self-creation" to many of the characters, narratives, subjects, actors, films, and filmmakers considered in this volume. The sampling of transgender films discussed in this introductory work reveals the enormous talent and dedication of filmmakers, actors, and other artists who have grappled with the complexity and profundity of a relatively new and yet timeless subject, with varying degrees of clarity, artistry and understanding. *Transgender Cinema* has scratched the surface of this field and suggested films for viewers' consideration, analysis, and—most of all—enjoyment. The astonishing variety of transgender films should spur readers to reconsider old favorites, taste a sampling of new films, and savor with wonder the contributions these films have made to our understanding of that curious and endlessly fascinating phenomenon we call gender.

ACKNOWLEDGMENTS

I am grateful for the privilege of writing on this fascinating subject for the Quick Takes series, and I wish to thank Gwendolyn Foster and Wheeler Winston Dixon for alerting me to this opportunity. Their encouragement and suggestions were invaluable in the process of developing and writing this volume. In a rapidly changing field, it is important to get information out in a readable format so that people can spread the word on developments in the ever-transforming world of media, and the publishers deserve recognition and kudos for offering this innovative format. I also thank Sally Angelica, who has worked with me as an editor, sounding board, researcher, and friend for years. I wish also to acknowledge the abiding influence of my dissertation director and friend, James Naremore, who first guided me as a superb dissertation director through the murky waters of androgyny in the early decades of my academic career. He advised me to write my dissertation as if it were just a book that was going to be published for a more popular audience—not as a dissertation. That is what I did, and Columbia University Press published that work in two editions entitled *Hollywood Androgyny*, guided by the excellent editing of William F. Bernhardt. I appreciate also the comments and suggestions from Victoria Smith, Jessica Soukup, and Sean Mardell at Texas State University. I am deeply grateful for the careful work of Andrew Katz and Rutgers University Press in bringing this work to fruition. I save my final and greatest appreciation for my beloved husband, Jean-Pierre Metereau, and our daughters, Marisa Bell-Metereau and Thea Bell-Metereau, who offer editing, encouragement, love, and models of organization, research, critical thinking, and tolerance as I write and revise. Thanks as well to all the other brilliant minds that contribute in countless other ways to my thinking and being in the world.

FURTHER READING

Barkin, Janna. *He's Always Been My Son: A Mother's Story about Raising Her Transgender Son*. London: Jessica Kingsley, 2017.

Blank, Hanne. *Straight: The Surprisingly Short History of Heterosexuality*. Boston: Beacon, 2012.

Charles, Casey. *Critical Queer Studies: Law, Film, and Fiction in Contemporary American Culture*. London: Taylor and Francis, 2016.

Deschamps, David, and Bennett L. Singer. *LGBTQ Stats: Lesbian, Gay, Bisexual, Transgender, and Queer People by the Numbers*. New York: New Press, 2017.

Eliason, Rachel. *The Agony, the Ecstasy and the Buddha: One Woman's Month in Thailand Having a Sex Change*. CreateSpace, 2017.

Fausto-Sterling, Anne. *Sexing the Body: Gender Politics and the Construction of Sexuality*. New York: Basic Books, 2000.

Feinberg, Leslie. *Transgender Warriors: Making History from Joan of Arc to Dennis Rodman*. Boston: Beacon, 2005.

Hwang, David Henry. *M. Butterfly: With an Afterword by the Playwright*. New York: Plume, 2006.

Joynt, Chase, and Michael Hoolboom. *You Only Live Twice: Sex, Death and Transition*. Toronto: Coach House Books, 2016.

Krieger, Irwin. *Counseling Transgender and Non-binary Youth: The Essential Guide*. London: Jessica Kingsley, 2017.

Lobdell, Bambi L. *"A Strange Sort of Being": The Transgender Life of Lucy Ann / Joseph Israel Lobdell, 1829–1912*. Jefferson, NC: McFarland, 2011.

Mardell, Ashley. *The ABC's of LGBT*. Coral Gables, FL: Mango Media, 2016.

Middlebrook, Diane Wood. *Suits Me: The Double Life of Billy Tipton*. Boston: Houghton Mifflin, 1999.

Nealy, Elijah C. *Transgender Children and Youth: Cultivating Pride and Joy with Families in Transition*. New York: Norton, 2017.

Nicolazzo, Z. *Trans* in College: Transgender Students' Strategies for Navigating Campus Life and the Institutional Politics of Inclusion*. Sterling, VA: Stylus, 2017.

Peele, Thomas. *Queer Popular Culture: Literature, Media, Film, and Television*. New York: Palgrave Macmillan, 2011.

Perper, Timothy, and Martha Cornog. *Mangatopia: Essays on Manga and Anime in the Modern World*. Santa Barbara, CA: Libraries Unlimited, 2011.

Sax, Leonard. *Why Gender Matters: What Parents and Teachers Need to Know about the Emerging Science of Sex Differences*. 2nd ed. New York: Harmony, 2017.

Shultz, Jackson Wright. *Trans/Portraits Voices from Transgender Communities*. Hanover, NH: Dartmouth College P, 2015.

Soukup, Jessica. *He/She/They-Us: Essential Information Vocabulary and Concepts to Help You Become a Better Ally to the Transgender and Gender Diverse People in Your Life*. Scottsdale, AZ: ICG Testing, 2017.

Stryker, Susan, and Erin Aizura, eds. *The Transgender Studies Reader*. Vol. 2. New York: Routledge, 2013.

Stryker, Susan, and Stephen Whittle, eds. *The Transgender Studies Reader*. Vol. 1. New York: Routledge, 2006.

Velasco, Sherry Marie. *The Lieutenant Nun: Transgenderism, Lesbian Desire, and Catalina De Erauso*. Austin: U of Texas P, 2000.

Wurst, Conchita. *Being Conchita: We Are Unstoppable*. London: John Blake, 2015.

WORKS CITED

Aaron, Michele. *New Queer Cinema: A Critical Reader*. New Brunswick, NJ: Rutgers UP, 2004.

"Are Phobos and Deimos Sailor Soldiers in Training?" *Tuxedo Unmasked* (blog) 6 Sept. 2018. Web. www.tuxedo unmasked.com/are-phobos-and-deimos-sailor-soldiers -in-training/.

Barclay, Barry. *Our Own Image*. Longman Paul, 1990.

Basoli, A. G. "Kimberly Peirce." *MovieMaker* 16 Nov. 1999. Web. https://web.archive.org/web/20150528224539/ http://www.moviemaker.com/archives/moviemaking/ directing/articles-directing/kimberly-peirce-3334/.

Bell, Christopher. "*Tomboy* Offers an Insight into Gender, Identity & Adolescence." *Indiewire* 14 Nov. 2011. Web. 17 Dec. 2017. www.indiewire.com/2011/11/review-tomboy -offers-an-insight-into-gender-identity-adolescence -115246/.

Bell-Metereau, Rebecca. *Hollywood Androgyny*. 2nd ed. New York: Columbia UP, 1993.

Brody, Jennifer Devere. "Boyz Do Cry: Screening History's White Lies." *Screen* 43.1 (March 2002): 91–96. Web. http://academic.oup.com/screen/article/43/1/91/ 1617158/Boyz-Do-Cry-screening-history-s-white-lies.

"Carlotta (1943–) performer." *Gender Variance Who's Who*

7 Sept 2010. Web. 21 Dec 2017. https://zagria.blogspot
.com/2010/09/carlotta-1943-performer.html#
.WlVBUktG2Rs.

Change over Time. Vimeo 2 Jan. 2018. http://vimeo.com/
66785175.

Coffman, Chris. "Woolf's *Orlando* and the Resonances of
Trans Studies." *Genders* 1 Feb. 2010. Web. www.colorado
.edu/gendersarchive1998-2013/2010/02/01/woolfs
-orlando-and-resonances-trans-studies.

Dannenbaum, Jed, Carroll Hodge, and Doe Mayer. *Creative
Filmmaking from the Inside Out: Five Keys to the Art of
Making Inspired Movies and Television*. New York: Simon
and Schuster, 2003.

Driver, Susan. *Queer Youth Cultures*. Albany: SUNY P, 2008.

Duarte, Ewan. "7 Independent Trans Filmmakers You
Ought to Know." *FTM Magazine* 10 Dec. 2016. Web.
http://ftmmagazine.com/7-independent-trans
-filmmakers-you-ought-to-know/.

Dubowsky, Jack Curtis. *Intersecting Film, Music, and Queer-
ness*. London: Palgrave, 2016.

Dunks, Glenn. "After Priscilla." *Metro*, no. 186 (Spring 2015):
26–31.

Ebert, Roger. "*Ma Vie en Rose*." *RogerEbert.com* 13 Feb. 1998.
Web. www.rogerebert.com/reviews/ma-vie-en-rose
-1998.

———. "*Tomboy*." *RogerEbert.com* 25 Jan. 2012. Web. www
.rogerebert.com/reviews/tomboy-2012.

Elbe, Lili. *Man into Woman: An Authentic Record of a Change
of Sex*. Ed. Niels Hoyer and Harthern Jacobson. Trans.
H. J Stenning. London: Jarrolds, 1933.

"Ellen." 8 Sept. 2015. *Gloublog*. Web. http://gloublog.net/ ?tag=ellen.

Farache, Emily. "Crying Foul over 'Boys Don't Cry.' " *E! News* 21 Oct. 1999. Web. www.eonline.com/news/38886/ crying-foul-over-boys-don-t-cry.

Green, Jesse. "Paris Has Burned." *New York Times* 17 Apr. 1993. Web. www.nytimes.com/1993/04/18/style/paris -has-burned.html.

Halberstam, Judith Jack. *In a Queer Time and Place: Trans- gender Bodies, Subcultural Lives*. New York: NYU P, 2005.

hooks, bell. *Black Looks: Race and Representation*. Boston: South End, 1992.

Humanity, Jon. "Charlie Chaplin—19th Century Tranny. 1889–1977." *YouTube* 4 Mar. 2017. Web. www.youtube .com/watch?v=TEuXSIdm4_A.

Johnson, Austin H. "Transnormativity: A New Concept and Its Validation through Documentary Film about Transgender Men." *Sociological Inquiry* 86.4 (June 2016): 465–91. Web. doi:10.1111/soin.12127.

Jong, Anneke. "You Can't Be What You Can't See: How to Get More Women in Tech." *The Muse* 23 Mar. 2012. Web. www.themuse.com/advice/you-cant-be-what-you-cant -see-how-to-get-more-women-in-tech.

Keegan, Cáel M. "History, Disrupted: The Aesthetic Gentri- fication of Queer and Trans Cinema." *Social Alternatives* 35.3 (July 2016): 50–56.

"List of Transgender Characters in Film and Television." *Wikipedia*. Web. 6 Jan. 2018. http://en.wikipedia.org/ wiki/List_of_transgender_characters_in_film_and_ television.

McCarthy, Nick. "Four Must-See Documentaries about Transgender Youth." *NBC News* 7 Mar. 2017. Web. www.nbcnews.com/feature/nbc-out/four-must-see-documentaries-about-transgender-youth-n730176.

Meyerowitz, Joanne J. *How Sex Changed: A History of Trans-sexuality in the United States.* Cambridge, MA: Harvard UP, 2009.

Morrison, Sara. "Covering the Transgender Community." *Nieman Reports* 70.1 (Winter 2016): 20–29.

Mulvey, Laura. *Death 24× a Second, Stillness and the Moving Image.* London: Reaktion Books, 2006.

Nicolson, Nigel. *Portrait of a Marriage: Vita Sackville-West and Harold Nicolson.* Chicago: U of Chicago P, 1973.

Olympic. "Meet the Transgender NCAA Swimmer from Harvard | Identify." *YouTube* 15 July 2017. Web. www.youtube.com/watch?v=niBM3Ii662U.

Ortega, Tony. "Kate's Amazing Voyage." *Village Voice* 2 May 2012. Web. http://digitalissue.villagevoice.com/article/Kate%27s+Amazing+Voyage/1051343/109965/article.html.

Ouditt, Sharon. "Coming across the Divide." *Adaptations: From Text to Screen, Screen to Text.* Ed. Deborah Cartmell and Imelda Whelehan. New York: Routledge, 2005. 146–56.

Peacefire. "CyberPatrol Examined." Web. 23 Oct. 2018. www.peacefire.org/censorware/Cyber_Patrol/.

Pelo, Ann. "Playing with Gender." *Rethinking Schools* Fall 2005. Web. www.rethinkingschools.org/articles/playing-with-gender.

Pidduck, Julianne. "The *Boys Don't Cry* Debate: Risk and Queer Spectatorship." *Screen* 42.1 (2001): 97–102. Web. doi:10.1093/screen/42.1.97.

Raymond, Janice G. *The Transsexual Empire: The Making of the She-Male*. New York: Teachers College P, 1994.

Roncero-Menendez, Sara. "Sailor Neptune and Uranus Come Out of the Fictional Closet." *Huffington Post* 2 Feb. 2016. Web. www.huffingtonpost.com/sara-roncero menendez/kissing-cousins-viz-wont-_b_5 353859.html.

Russell, N'Donna. "What Sailor Moon Means to Women All over the World." *Public Radio International* 27 June 2015. Web. www.pri.org/stories/2015-06-27/what-sailor -moon-means-women-all-over-world.

Ryan, Joelle Ruby. "Diversifying and Complicating Representations of Trans Lives: Five Documentaries about Gender Identity." *Feminist Collections: A Quarterly of Women's Studies Resources* 5.3 (2010): 10–16.

"Sailor Moon Graphic Novels Top Bookstore Sales." *ICv2: The Business of Geek Culture* 13 Aug. 2001. Web. https:// icv2.com/articles/comics/view/625/sailor-moon -graphic-novels-top-bookstore-sales.

"Sailor Moon TV Series Full Cast & Crew." *IMDb*. Web. 14 Dec. 2017. www.imdb.com/title/tt0114327/fullcredits ?ref_=tt_cl_sm#cast.

Sanjek, David. "The Doll and The Whip: Pathos and Bally-hoo in William Castle's *Homicidal*." *Quarterly Review of Film and Video* 20.4 (2003): 247–63.

Sarris, Andrew. *The Films of Josef von Sternberg*. New York: Doubleday, 1966.

Schulman, Sarah. *The Gentrification of the Mind: Witness to a Lost Imagination*. Berkeley: U of California P, 2002.

Scott, A. O. "Review: *A Fantastic Woman* Lives Up to Its Title, in More Ways than One." *New York Times* 15 Nov. 2017. Web. www.nytimes.com/2017/11/15/movies/a -fantastic-woman-review.html.

Sontag, Susan. *Against Interpretation and Other Essays*. New York: Macmillan, 2001.

Vanaerde, Sigourney. "Yuri or Kissing Cousins: Gender and Resistance to Heteronormative Society in Sailor Moon." Unpublished essay, Texas State U, 2017.

Vigo, Julian. "Dispelling Fictions and Disrupting Hashtags." *Counterpunch* 25 Aug. 2014. Web. www.counterpunch .org/2014/08/25/dispelling-fictions-and-disrupting -hashtags/.

Villa, Sara. "The Photograph, the Portrait and Orlando's Double Nature." *Culture* 19 (2005–6): 189–98. Web. 21 Aug. 2017. https://air.unimi.it/retrieve/handle/2434/ 211087/251499/Ebookculture2005-2006.pdf#page=189.

Wood, Robin. "An Introduction to the American Horror Film." *Movies and Methods*. Vol. 2. Ed. Bill Nichols. Berkeley: U of California P, 1985. 195–219.

Woodward, Suzanne. "Being Both: Gender and Indigeneity in Two Pacific Documentary Films." *Pacific Journalism Review* 21.2 (2015): 63–77. Web. doi:10.24135/pjr.v21i2.117.

Woolf, Virginia. *The Essays of Virginia Woolf*. Volume 4: *1925–28*. London: Hogarth, 1994.

York, Ashley. "Becoming Chaz (Feature Documentary Field Director & Producer)." *Vimeo* 2012. Web. https://vimeo .com/44969475.

SELECTED FILMOGRAPHY

Adventures of Priscilla, Queen of the Desert. Dir. Stephan Elliott. U.S., 1994.

All about My Mother. Dir. Pedro Almodóvar. Spain, 1999.

Alto. Dir. Nikki del Monico. U.S., 2015.

Anak. Dir. Rory Quintos. Philippines, 2000.

Austin Unbound. Dir. Eliza Greenwood and Sel Stanley. U.S., 2011.

Becoming Chaz. Dir. Fenton Bailey and Randy Barbato. U.S., 2011.

Blossoming of Maximo Oliveros, The. Dir. Auraeus Solito. Philippines, 2007.

Boy I Am. Dir. Sam Feder and Julie Hollar. U.S., 2006.

Boy Meets Girl. Dir. Eric Schaeffer. U.S., 2014.

Boys Don't Cry. Dir. Kimberly Peirce. U.S., 1999.

Brandon Teena Story, The. Dir. Susan Muska and Gréta Olafsdóttir. U.S., 1998.

Busy Day, A. Dir. Mack Sennett. U.S., 1915.

Call Me Malcolm. Dir. Joseph Parlagreco. U.S., 2005.

Carlotta. Dir. Samantha Lang. Australia, 2014.

Change over Time. Dir. Ewan Duarte. 2013.

Crying Game, The. Dir. Neil Jordan. UK, 1992.

Dallas Buyers Club. Dir. Jean-Marc Vallée. U.S., 2013.

Danish Girl, The. Dir. Tom Hooper. U.S., 2015.

Devil Is a Woman, The. U.S., 1935.

Drunktown's Finest. Dir. Sydney Freeland. U.S., 2014.

Facing Mirrors. Dir. Negar Azarbayjani. Iran, 2011.

Fantastic Woman, A. Dir. Sebastián Lelio. Chile, 2017.

52 Tuesdays. Dir. Sophie Hyde. Australia, 2013.

Flesh. Dir. Andy Warhol. U.S., 1968.

Girl Inside. Dir. Maya Gallus. Canada, 2007.

Girl like Me, A: The Gwen Araujo Story. Dir. Agnieszka Holland. U.S., 2006.

Hedwig and the Angry Inch. Dir. John Cameron Mitchell. U.S., 2001.

I Was a Male War Bride. Dir. Howard Hawks. U.S., 1949.

Kate Bornstein Is a Queer and Pleasant Danger. Dir. Sam Feder. U.S., 2014.

Kumu Hina. Dir. Dean Hamer and Joe Wilson. U.S., 2014.

La Cage aux Folles. Dir. Édouard Molinaro. France, 1978.

Ma Vie en Rose (My life in pink). Dir. Alain Berliner. France, 1997.

Masquerader, The. Dir. Charlie Chaplin. U.S., 1914.

Myra Breckinridge. Dir. Mike Sarne. U.S., 1970.

Orlando. Dir. Sally Potter. UK, 1993.

Paris Is Burning. Dir. Jennie Livingston. U.S., 1991.

Playing with Gender. Dir. Ashley Altadonna. U.S., 2007.

Psycho. Dir. Alfred Hitchcock. U.S., 1960.

Queen Christina. Dir. Rouben Mamoulian. U.S., 1933.

Rocky Horror Picture Show, The. Dir. Jim Sharman. 1975.

Saga of Anatahan, The. Dir. Josef von Sternberg. Japan, 1954.

She's a Boy I Knew. Dir. Gwen Hayworth. Canada, 2007.

Silence of the Lambs. Dir. Jonathan Demme. 1991.

Some Like It Hot. Dir. Billy Wilder. U.S., 1959.

Southern Comfort. Dir. Kate Davis. U.S., 2001.

Still Black: A Portrait of Black Transmen. Dir. Kortney Ryan
    Ziegler. U.S., 2008.

Stonewall. Dir. Roland Emmerich. Germany, 2015.

Tenant, The. Dir. Roman Polanski. U.S., 1976.

Three Generations. Dir. Gaby Dellal. Brazil, 2015.

Tomboy. Céline Sciamma. France, 2011.

Tootsie. Dir. Sydney Pollack. U.S., 1982.

Transamerica. Dir. Duncan Tucker. U.S., 2005.

Transparent. Dir. Jules Rosskam. U.S., 2005.

Trash. Dir. Andy Warhol. U.S., 1970.

Whatever Suits You. Dir. Ashley Altadonna. U.S., 2007.

Woman, A. Dir. Charlie Chaplin. U.S., 1915.

INDEX

ABOUT THE AUTHOR

Rebecca Bell-Metereau teaches film and directs the Media Studies minor at Texas State University. A Fulbright Scholar and winner of the Texas State Award for Excellence in Service and Alumni and Faculty Senate Awards for Excellence in Teaching, she has served as the special assistant to the Texas State president and director of the Ford Foundation–ISM Diversity and Media grant. She is the author of *Hollywood Androgyny* (two editions), the coauthor of *Simone Weil on Politics Religion and Society*, and the coeditor of *Star Bodies and the Erotics of Suffering*, as well as having contributed many essays to edited volumes and journals.